ESSYWRITES PRESS

Dummies Guide to Starting Your Own Business

Essential Steps to Launching and Scaling a Successful Small Business Venture

First edition

This book was professionally typeset on Reedsy.
Find out more at reedsy.com

Contents

INTRODUCTION

Every great journey begins with a single, often humble step. My own entrepreneurial story started with something as simple as journaling. As the Lead Writer for EssyWrites Press, my journey into the world of business and writing began with a simple act: journaling. What started as a personal endeavor to capture my thoughts, dreams, and daily experiences gradually transformed into a profound passion for storytelling and sharing knowledge. This passion became the foundation of EssyWrites Press. This venture has grown from humble beginnings to a successful enterprise with a team of dedicated editors and a series of best-selling books available both online and offline.

Years ago, as I sat at my desk, filling the pages of my journal, I never imagined that those simple entries would lead me to where I am today. Each page was a step forward, a moment of reflection, and an opportunity to explore new ideas. Writing became a way for me to understand the world and my place within it. This introspective journey sparked a desire to help others find their voices and share their stories.

As my journaling habit grew, so did my vision. I realized that there were countless individuals out there with stories to tell, ideas to share, and dreams to pursue. I wanted to create a platform where these voices could be heard and where aspiring writers could find the support and resources they needed to succeed. And so, EssyWrites Press was born.

Key Motivations for Starting Your Business

Like me, many people are driven by powerful motivations to start their businesses. The desire for independence, the pursuit of passion, and the aspiration to make a difference are just a few reasons why individuals leap into entrepreneurship.

Independence and Control: Owning a business offers the freedom to be your boss, make your own decisions, and shape your destiny. It allows you to break free from the constraints of traditional employment and create a life that aligns with your values and goals.

Passion and Purpose: At the heart of many successful businesses is a deep-seated passion. Entrepreneurs often turn their hobbies, interests, or expertise into ventures that bring them joy and fulfillment. This passion fuels their perseverance and creativity, driving them to overcome obstacles and achieve their dreams.

Financial Potential: While financial gain is not the sole motivation, the potential for profit and financial security are significant factors. Building a successful business can provide economic stability and the opportunity for wealth creation, allowing you to support yourself and your loved ones.

Making a Difference: Entrepreneurs have the power to create positive change in their communities and beyond. By addressing unmet needs, solving problems, and innovating, they can make a lasting impact and contribute to the betterment of society.

Personal Growth and Challenge: The journey of entrepreneurship is a path of continuous learning and self-discovery. It challenges you to develop new skills, adapt to changing circumstances, and push beyond your comfort zone. This personal growth is often as rewarding as the business success itself.

How This Book Will Guide Readers Through Their Entrepreneurial Journey.

Embarking on the entrepreneurial journey can be both exhilarating and daunting. Like me, you may have a vision and the passion to pursue it, but the path to success is often fraught with challenges and uncertainties. This book is designed to be your trusted companion, providing you with the knowledge, tools, and inspiration you need to navigate the complexities of starting and scaling a successful small business.

Step-by-Step Guidance: This book breaks down the entrepreneurial process into manageable steps, offering clear and actionable advice at each stage. From identifying your business idea to crafting a comprehensive business plan, securing funding, and launching your venture, you will find practical tips and strategies to guide you.

Real-Life Examples and Case Studies: Learning from the experiences of others can be incredibly valuable. Throughout this book, you will find real-life examples and case studies of successful entrepreneurs who have walked the path before you. Their stories will provide insights, lessons, and inspiration, helping you to avoid common pitfalls and make informed decisions.

Actionable Checklists and Templates: To ensure that you can apply what you learn, this book includes actionable checklists and templates. These tools will help you organize your thoughts, track your progress, and stay focused on your goals.

Practical Tools and Resources: In addition to the guidance provided in the chapters, this book offers a wealth of practical tools and resources. From financial planning software to marketing strategies and legal considerations, you will have access to the information you need to build a strong foundation for your business.

Simplified Language and Accessible Format: Recognizing that not everyone comes from a business background, this book is written in clear and simple language. Jargon is minimized, and complex concepts are explained in an accessible way, ensuring that you can easily grasp and apply the information.

Continuous Support and Community Engagement: Your entrepreneurial journey doesn't end with the launch of your business. This book emphasizes the importance of continuous learning and adaptation. It also encourages you to engage with the entrepreneurial community, offering resources for networking, mentorship, and ongoing education.

Overview of the Chapters and What Readers Can Expect to Learn.

This book is structured to take you from the initial spark of an idea through to the successful operation and growth of your business. Here's a brief overview of the chapters and what you can expect to learn:

Building Confidence and Overcoming Fear: Learn how to tackle the fear of failure, embrace uncertainty, and invest in personal growth to build the confidence needed for entrepreneurial success.

Identifying and Validating Your Business Idea: Discover techniques for generating business ideas, conducting SWOT analysis, and spotting market opportunities. Learn how to evaluate ideas using the R.O.I. concept and explore cost-effective business examples.

Funding Your Business: Explore various funding sources, including loans, investments, and grants. Learn how to bootstrap your business with minimal resources and manage your finances effectively.

Developing Your Business Plan: Understand the essential elements of a business plan and learn how to craft an engaging executive summary, conduct market research, and create financial projections. This chapter includes a detailed example of a business plan.

Legal Setup and Registration: Navigate the legal requirements for business registration, choose the right business structure, and ensure legal compliance. Learn how to set up business bank accounts and obtain an EIN.

Building and Testing Your Minimum Viable Product (MVP): Understand the MVP concept and learn how to identify and develop key features. Explore real-life examples and learn how to iterate and improve based on feedback.

Branding and Marketing Strategies: Develop a strong brand identity and craft a unique selling proposition. Learn effective marketing strategies, including social media and digital marketing, SEO basics, and the pros and cons of different advertising platforms.

Sales and Customer Relationship Management: Build a robust sales strategy and master techniques for excellent customer service. Learn how to handle customer feedback and create loyal customers and advocates.

Accounting and Financial Management: Set up an efficient accounting system, choose the right software, and manage cash flow and expenses. Understand key financial reports and their importance.

Growing and Scaling Your Business: Discover strategies for business expansion, adding new products or services, and entering new markets. Learn best practices for recruiting and managing employees and forming strategic partnerships.

Continuous Learning and Adaptation: Stay updated with market trends and overcome common business challenges. Embrace continuous learning and access to resources for ongoing education and networking.

Real-World Success Stories and Final Thoughts: Gain inspiration from the stories of successful entrepreneurs and learn from their failures and triumphs. Recap key takeaways and find encouragement for your entrepreneurial journey.

Appendices: Access essential checklists and templates, a glossary of business terms, recommended reading, and online tools for additional support.

Chapter 1: Debunking Common Entrepreneurship Myths with Real Life Stories.

Starting a business is an exciting journey, but it's often surrounded by myths that can create unnecessary fears or false expectations. To help you navigate your entrepreneurial path with clarity and confidence, let's debunk some of the most common myths about starting a business.

Myth 1: You Need a Lot of Money to Start a Business

One of the most pervasive myths is that you need a significant amount of capital to start a business. While funding is essential, it's not always necessary to have a large sum of money upfront.

Sara Blakely, the founder of Spanx, started her billion-dollar company with just $5,000 in savings. She used her initial investment wisely, focusing on developing a prototype and securing a patent before launching her product. Blakely's story demonstrates that with creativity and resourcefulness, you can start a successful business with limited funds.

Myth 2: You Must Have a Perfect Business Plan

Another common myth is that you need a flawless business plan before starting your business. While planning is crucial, waiting for a perfect plan can lead to paralysis by analysis.

Drew Houston, the co-founder of Dropbox, initially launched a simple demo video to validate his idea. Instead of spending months on a detailed business plan, he focused on proving the concept and gathering feedback. This approach allowed Dropbox to iterate quickly and attract early adopters.

Myth 3: You Have to Quit Your Day Job

Many aspiring entrepreneurs believe they must quit their day job to start a business. However, maintaining a steady income while building your venture can provide financial stability and reduce stress.

Craig Newmark, the founder of Craigslist, started the platform as a side project while working full-time as a software engineer. By gradually building his business, he was able to scale Craigslist into one of the most popular classified ad websites globally.

Myth 4: You Need to Be an Expert in Your Industry

It's a common misconception that you need extensive industry experience to succeed in business. While knowledge is beneficial, passion, adaptability, and a willingness to learn are often more critical.

The founders of Airbnb, Brian Chesky, and Joe Gebbia, had yet to gain experience in the hospitality industry when they started. Their background in design helped them approach the business creatively, and their determination to learn and adapt contributed significantly to their success.

Myth 5: Failure Means the End

Failure is often seen as the end of the road, but in entrepreneurship, it's usually just a stepping stone to success. Many successful entrepreneurs have faced failures before achieving their goals.

Colonel Harland Sanders, the founder of KFC, faced numerous rejections and failures before his chicken recipe gained popularity. He started KFC in his 60s after being turned down by over 1,000 restaurants. His persistence paid off, and KFC became a global brand.

Building a Success-Oriented Mindset

A success-oriented mindset is crucial for navigating the ups and downs of entrepreneurship. It shapes how you approach challenges, make decisions, and persevere in the face of adversity.

Why is Mindset Important for Business Success?

1. Resilience in Adversity: A positive mindset helps you stay resilient when faced with obstacles. Instead of seeing challenges as insurmountable, you view them as opportunities to learn and grow.

2. Proactive Decision-Making: Entrepreneurs with a success-oriented mindset are proactive. They take initiative, seek solutions, and make informed decisions that drive their business forward.

3. Adaptability: The business landscape is constantly changing. A flexible mindset allows you to adapt to new circumstances, pivot when necessary, and seize emerging opportunities.

4. Motivation and Persistence: Building and running a business requires sustained effort. A positive mindset keeps you motivated, helping you persist through difficult times and maintain your drive to succeed.

Practical Strategies to Build a Success-Oriented Mindset

1. Embrace a Growth Mindset

A growth mindset, as defined by psychologist Carol Dweck, is the belief that abilities and intelligence can be developed through effort, learning, and persistence. Embracing a growth mindset can transform how you approach your business.

3

- **Focus on Learning**: View challenges as learning opportunities. Every setback is a chance to gain new insights and improve.
- **Seek Feedback**: Actively seek feedback from mentors, peers, and customers. Use it constructively to refine your strategies and grow.
- **Celebrate Effort, Not Just Success**: Acknowledge the hard work and effort you put into your business, regardless of the outcome.

2. Set Clear Goals

Setting clear, achievable goals provides direction and purpose. It helps you stay focused and measure your progress.

- **SMART Goals**: Ensure your goals are Specific, Measurable, Achievable, Relevant, and Time-bound. For example, instead of saying, "I want to grow my business," set a goal like, "I want to increase my monthly revenue by 20% within the next six months."
- **Break Down Goals:** Divide larger goals into smaller, manageable tasks. This makes them less daunting and helps you maintain momentum.

3. Practice Positive Thinking

Positive thinking can significantly impact your mindset and overall outlook on life. It doesn't mean ignoring challenges but approaching them with optimism.

- **Affirmations**: Use positive affirmations to reinforce your confidence and self-belief. For example, start your day with affirmations like, "I am capable of achieving my goals" or "I can overcome any challenge."
- **Gratitude**: Cultivate a habit of gratitude. Regularly reflect on the positive aspects of your journey, no matter how small they may seem.

4. Surround Yourself with Positive Influences

The people you surround yourself with can greatly influence your mindset. Build a support network of positive, like-minded individuals.

- **Mentors**: Seek out mentors who can provide guidance, support, and inspiration. Their experience and advice can be invaluable.
- **Peer Groups:** Join entrepreneurial groups or networks where you can share experiences, exchange ideas, and receive encouragement.

5. Maintain Work-Life Balance

Burnout can negatively affect your mindset and overall well-being. Strive to maintain a healthy work-life balance.

- **Schedule Downtime**: Allocate time for rest, relaxation, and activities you enjoy outside of work. This helps recharge your energy and creativity.
- **Delegate Tasks**: Learn to delegate tasks to your team or outsource them. This allows you to focus on high-impact activities and reduces stress.

Checklist for Developing a Positive Entrepreneurial Mindset

1. Adopt a Growth Mindset
- View challenges as opportunities for growth.
- Seek continuous learning and improvement.
- Celebrate effort and progress.

2. Set Clear Goals
- Define SMART goals for your business.
- Break down large goals into smaller tasks.
- Regularly review and adjust your goals.

3. Practice Positive Thinking
- Use daily affirmations to boost confidence.
- Reflect on positive experiences and achievements.
- Cultivate gratitude.

4. Build a Support Network
- Connect with mentors and seek their guidance.

- Join entrepreneurial groups and networks.
- Surround yourself with positive, like-minded individuals.

5. Maintain Work-Life Balance

- Schedule regular downtime and relaxation.
- Delegate tasks to reduce workload.
- Engage in hobbies and activities outside of work.

6. Stay Adaptable

- Be open to change and new ideas.
- Embrace flexibility in your business strategies.
- Learn from failures and use them as stepping stones.

7. Develop Resilience

- Focus on solutions rather than problems.
- Maintain persistence and determination.
- Learn to manage stress effectively.

8. Seek Feedback and Act on It

- Regularly solicit feedback from customers, peers, and mentors.
- Use feedback constructively to make improvements.
- Implement changes based on insights gained.

9. Celebrate Small Wins

- Acknowledge and celebrate your achievements, no matter how small.
- Use milestones to motivate and inspire further progress.
- Share successes with your team and support network.

By debunking common entrepreneurship myths and building a success-oriented mindset, you're setting the foundation for a thriving business. Remember, the journey of entrepreneurship is as much about personal growth as it is about business success. Embrace the challenges, learn from every experience, and stay committed to your vision. With the right mindset, there's no limit to what you can achieve.

CHAPTER 2: PREPARING FOR YOUR ENTREPRENEURIAL JOURNEY

BUILDING CONFIDENCE AND OVERCOMING FEAR

Starting a business is a bold and transformative step. It promises new opportunities, the potential for financial independence, and the satisfaction of turning your passion into a profession. However, the journey also comes with its fair share of fears and uncertainties. Understanding these fears and learning how to overcome them is crucial to building the confidence necessary for entrepreneurial success.

Common Fears Associated with Starting a Business

Fear of Failure: The fear of failure is perhaps the most prevalent concern among aspiring entrepreneurs. It stems from the uncertainty of whether the business will succeed, the potential financial losses, and the impact on personal and professional reputation.

Fear of Financial Instability: Starting a business often requires significant financial investment, and the fear of financial instability can be overwhelming. Concerns about securing funding, managing cash flow, and the possibility of debt weigh heavily on many entrepreneurs.

Fear of the Unknown: The entrepreneurial journey is filled with unknowns. From market conditions to customer preferences, the lack of certainty can be daunting. The unpredictable nature of business environments compounds this fear.

Fear of Inadequacy: Many potential entrepreneurs doubt their abilities and worry that they lack the necessary skills, knowledge, or experience to run a successful business. This fear of inadequacy can be paralyzing and prevent individuals from taking the first step.

Fear of Rejection: Fear of rejection, whether from potential investors, customers, or even friends and family, can deter individuals from pursuing their business ideas. The possibility of others not believing in their vision is a significant concern.

Fear of Losing Work-Life Balance: The demands of starting and running a business can impact personal life. The fear of losing work-life balance, sacrificing family time, and personal well-being is a common worry.

Actionable Steps to Overcome the Fear of Failure

Overcoming fear, especially the fear of failure requires a combination of mind-set shifts, practical strategies, and continuous effort. Here are actionable steps to help you build confidence and face your entrepreneurial journey with courage:

Reframe Failure as a Learning Opportunity

Instead of viewing failure as a negative outcome, reframe it as a valuable learning experience. Every setback provides insights that can guide you toward better decisions and strategies in the future.

Action Step: Reflect on past failures and identify what you learned from them. Write down these lessons and how they can be applied to your current entrepreneurial journey.

9

Set Realistic and Achievable Goals

Break down your larger business objectives into smaller, manageable goals. Achieving these smaller milestones can boost your confidence and provide a sense of progress.

Action Step: Create a list of short-term goals that align with your long-term vision. Celebrate each milestone as you achieve it.

Conduct Thorough Research and Planning

Knowledge reduces uncertainty. Conducting thorough market research and creating a detailed business plan can provide clarity and reduce the fear of the unknown.

Action Step: Develop a comprehensive business plan that includes market analysis, financial projections, and a clear strategy for growth.

Build a Support Network

Surround yourself with supportive and like-minded individuals. Mentors, advisors, and fellow entrepreneurs can provide guidance, encouragement, and valuable feedback.

Action Step: Join entrepreneurial networks, attend industry events, and seek out mentors who can offer support and advice.

Improve Your Skills and Knowledge

Invest in your personal and professional development. The more competent and knowledgeable you feel, the more confident you will be in your abilities.

Action Step: Enroll in relevant courses, attend workshops, and read books on entrepreneurship and your specific industry.

Prepare Financially

Financial worries can be mitigated by careful planning and preparation. Create a detailed budget, explore funding options, and build a financial cushion to manage initial uncertainties.

Action Step: Consult with a financial advisor to develop a realistic budget and financial plan for your business.

Embrace a Positive Mindset

Cultivate a positive and resilient mindset. Practice self-affirmation, visualize success, and focus on your strengths.

Action Step: Start each day with positive affirmations and visualize the successful outcomes of your efforts.

Take Small Steps

You don't have to take a giant leap all at once. Start with small, manageable steps that gradually build toward your larger goals.

Action Step: Identify one small action you can take today to move your business idea forward and commit to doing it.

Case Study: Overcoming Significant Challenges

The Story of Howard Schultz and Starbucks

Howard Schultz's journey with Starbucks is a powerful example of overcoming significant challenges and the fear of failure. Schultz grew up in a poor family in Brooklyn, New York. Despite his difficult upbringing, he earned a degree in Communications and initially worked in sales and marketing. His entrepreneurial journey began when he joined Starbucks, which was a small coffee bean retailer at the time.

Challenge 1: Convincing Investors

When Schultz first presented his idea to transform Starbucks into a coffeehouse chain, he faced significant resistance. Investors were skeptical about his vision of creating a "third place" between home and work where people could relax and enjoy high-quality coffee. Many believed that the American market wouldn't embrace the European-style coffee culture.

Action Taken: Schultz's unwavering belief in his vision and his ability to articulate it convincingly eventually won over investors. He continued to pitch his idea relentlessly, refining his presentation and addressing concerns until he secured the necessary funding.

Lesson: Persistence and a clear, compelling vision can help overcome initial skepticism and resistance.

Challenge 2: Financial Struggles

In the early years, Starbucks faced significant financial challenges. The company struggled with cash flow issues, and Schultz had to make difficult decisions, including laying off employees and closing stores. These challenges tested his resilience and belief in his vision.

Action Taken: Schultz focused on improving operational efficiency, cutting unnecessary costs, and optimizing the supply chain. He also took bold steps to innovate, such as introducing new products and expanding the menu to attract a broader customer base.

Lesson: Financial challenges are a common part of entrepreneurship. Addressing them with strategic planning, cost management, and innovation can lead to recovery and growth.

Challenge 3: Navigating Market Expansion

As Starbucks expanded globally, it faced cultural and market-specific challenges. Adapting the brand to different markets while maintaining its core identity requires careful navigation.

Action Taken: Schultz and his team conducted extensive market research to understand local preferences and behaviors. They adapted store designs, menu offerings, and marketing strategies to resonate with local customers while preserving the Starbucks brand essence.

Lesson: Successful market expansion requires a balance between adapting to local cultures and maintaining brand consistency.

Challenge 4: Leadership Transition

In 2000, Schultz stepped down as CEO, believing the company was in good hands. However, Starbucks faced declining performance and brand dilution during his absence. The company struggled with over-expansion and losing its connection with customers.

Action Taken: Schultz returned as CEO in 2008, making tough decisions to close underperforming stores and refocus on quality and customer experience. He redefined the company's mission and values, reigniting the passion that had initially driven Starbucks' success.

Lesson: Strong leadership and a clear vision are essential for navigating crises and revitalizing a brand.

Challenge 5: Personal Sacrifices

Throughout his journey, Schultz faced personal sacrifices and the pressure of balancing business demands with family life. The intense workload and stress took a toll on his well-being.

Action Taken: Schultz learned to delegate responsibilities, build a strong leadership team, and prioritize his health and family. He emphasized the importance of work-life balance for himself and his employees.

Lesson: Achieving a healthy work-life balance is crucial for sustainable success and personal well-being.

Howard Schultz's journey with Starbucks illustrates that fear and challenges are inherent parts of the entrepreneurial journey. Overcoming these fears requires persistence, strategic thinking, and a resilient mindset. Schultz's story is proof of the power of believing in your vision, adapting to changing circumstances, and continuously learning from experiences.

Checklist for Overcoming Fear and Building Confidence

1. Reframe Failure as a Learning Opportunity
- Reflect on past failures and identify lessons learned.
- View setbacks as opportunities for growth and improvement.

2. Set Realistic and Achievable Goals
- Create short-term goals that align with your long-term vision.
- Celebrate each milestone to boost confidence.

3. Conduct Thorough Research and Planning
- Develop a comprehensive business plan with market analysis and financial projections.
- Use research to reduce uncertainty and clarify your strategy.

4. Build a Support Network
- Join entrepreneurial networks and seek mentors for guidance.
- Surround yourself with supportive, like-minded individuals.

5. Improve Your Skills and Knowledge
- Invest in personal and professional development through courses and workshops.
- Continuously seek new knowledge relevant to your industry.

6. Prepare Financially
- Create a detailed budget and explore funding options.
- Build a financial cushion to manage initial uncertainties.

7. Embrace a Positive Mindset
- Practice daily affirmations and visualize success.
- Cultivate gratitude and focus on positive experiences.

8. Take Small Steps

- Identify one small action to move your business idea forward.
- Gradually build momentum with manageable tasks.

Embracing Uncertainty

Why is Uncertainty a Part of Entrepreneurship?

Uncertainty is an inherent aspect of entrepreneurship. When starting and running a business, you face countless unknowns and variables that can influence outcomes in unpredictable ways. Here are a few reasons why uncertainty is so integral to the entrepreneurial journey:

1. **Market Dynamics:** Markets are constantly changing due to factors like consumer preferences, technological advancements, and economic shifts. These changes create a dynamic environment where entrepreneurs must continuously adapt.

2. **Innovation and Competition**: Entrepreneurs often venture into uncharted territories with innovative products or services. This innovation is accompanied by the uncertainty of how the market will respond and how competitors will react.

3. **Financial Risks:** Starting and scaling a business involves financial investments that may not yield immediate returns. The uncertainty of cash flow, funding, and profitability is a significant challenge.

4. **Regulatory Changes**: Businesses must navigate a complex web of regulations and policies, which can change unexpectedly and impact operations.

5. **Resource Limitations:** Entrepreneurs frequently operate with limited resources, including time, money, and manpower. The uncertainty of resource availability adds complexity to decision-making.

How Can Embracing Uncertainty Lead to Growth and Innovation?

Embracing uncertainty doesn't mean ignoring risks or acting recklessly. Instead, it involves accepting the unpredictable nature of business and leveraging it for growth and innovation. Here's how embracing uncertainty can be beneficial:

1. **Encourages Creativity and Innovation**: Uncertainty challenges entrepreneurs to think outside the box and develop creative solutions. When the future is unpredictable, innovative approaches can provide a competitive edge.

2. **Fosters Resilience**: Dealing with uncertainty builds resilience. Entrepreneurs learn to navigate challenges, recover from setbacks, and remain adaptable in the face of adversity.

3. **Promotes Agility:** Embracing uncertainty requires a flexible mindset and the ability to pivot quickly. Agile businesses can respond more effectively to market changes and capitalize on emerging opportunities.

4. **Drives Continuous Improvement**: Uncertainty keeps entrepreneurs on their toes, encouraging continuous learning and improvement. This proactive approach ensures that businesses remain relevant and competitive.

5. **Opens New Opportunities:** Uncertainty often uncovers new opportunities that wouldn't have been visible in a more predictable environment. Entrepreneurs who embrace uncertainty are better positioned to identify and seize these opportunities.

Checklist for Managing Uncertainty in Business

1. Develop a Flexible Business Plan

- Regularly review and update your business plan to reflect changes in the market and your business environment.

- Include contingency plans to address potential risks and uncertainties.

2. Stay Informed

- Keep up with industry trends, market conditions, and regulatory changes.

- Engage with industry experts, attend conferences, and read relevant publications.

3. Build a Strong Network

- Cultivate relationships with mentors, advisors, and other entrepreneurs.

- Leverage your network for support, advice, and collaboration opportunities.

4. Diversify Revenue Streams

- Explore multiple revenue streams to reduce dependence on a single source of income.

- Diversification can provide financial stability and mitigate risk.

5. Invest in Innovation

- Foster a culture of innovation within your business.

- Encourage experimentation and support new ideas, even if they come with some risk.

6. Maintain Financial Reserves

- Build a financial cushion to manage cash flow fluctuations and unexpected expenses.

- Regularly review your financial health and make adjustments as needed.

7. Focus on Agility

- Develop agile business processes that allow for quick decision-making and adaptation.
- Encourage a flexible mindset within your team.

8. Embrace a Learning Culture

- Promote continuous learning and professional development for yourself and your team.
- Encourage feedback and use it to drive improvement.

9. Accept and Manage Risks

- Conduct regular risk assessments to identify potential threats and opportunities.
- Implement risk management strategies to mitigate the impact of uncertainties.

10. Maintain a Positive Outlook

- Cultivate a positive mindset and focus on opportunities rather than challenges.
- Use positive affirmations and visualize successful outcomes.

Investing in Personal Growth

How Does Personal Development Contribute to Business Success?

Personal development is the process of improving your skills, knowledge, and mindset to reach your full potential. In the context of entrepreneurship, personal development is crucial for several reasons:

1. Enhances Leadership Skills: Effective leadership is vital for guiding your business and inspiring your team. Personal development helps you build essential leadership qualities such as communication, decision-making, and emotional intelligence.

2. Boosts Confidence and Resilience: Building your skills and knowledge boosts your confidence, enabling you to tackle challenges with a positive attitude. Resilience, developed through personal growth, helps you bounce back from setbacks.

3. Improves Problem-Solving Abilities: Personal development enhances critical thinking and problem-solving skills. These abilities are essential for navigating the complexities of running a business.

4. Encourages Innovation and Creativity: Exposure to new ideas and perspectives through personal growth activities can spark creativity and innovation, leading to unique solutions and business strategies.

5. Fosters Better Relationships: Personal development often includes improving interpersonal skills, which can help you build stronger relationships with employees, customers, and business partners.

6. Increases Productivity and Efficiency: Developing time management and organizational skills can lead to better productivity and efficiency, helping you achieve your business goals more effectively.

Practical Steps for Investing in Personal Growth

1. Set Clear Personal Development Goals

- Identify the areas where you want to grow and set specific, measurable, achievable, relevant, and time-bound (SMART) goals.
- For example, you might set a goal to improve your public speaking skills by attending a workshop within the next three months.

2. Create a Personal Development Plan

- Outline the steps you will take to achieve your goals, including the resources and time required.

- Break down your plan into manageable tasks and set deadlines to stay on track.

3. Seek Continuous Learning Opportunities

- Enroll in courses, attend workshops, and participate in seminars related to your areas of interest.
- Consider both formal education and informal learning opportunities, such as online courses and webinars.

4. Read Widely

- Read books, articles, and journals on topics relevant to your personal and professional growth.
- Explore a variety of genres and subjects to gain diverse perspectives and insights.

5. Network with Like-Minded Individuals

- Join professional associations, networking groups, and online communities to connect with other entrepreneurs and professionals.
- Attend industry events, conferences, and meetups to expand your network and learn from others.

6. Find a Mentor

- Seek out a mentor who can provide guidance, support, and valuable insights based on their experiences.
- Build a relationship with your mentor through regular meetings and open communication.

7. Practice Self-Reflection

- Regularly reflect on your experiences, successes, and areas for improvement.
- Use journaling or mindfulness practices to gain insights into your thoughts, emotions, and behaviors.

8. Embrace Feedback

- Actively seek feedback from colleagues, mentors, and customers to identify areas for growth.
- Use feedback constructively to make improvements and enhance your skills.

9. Stay Open to Change

- Embrace change and be willing to adapt your goals and strategies as needed.
- Stay flexible and open-minded to new ideas and opportunities for growth.

Building Confidence Through Personal Development

As you embrace uncertainty and commit to personal growth, you'll find that your confidence naturally begins to build. This confidence is not just a byproduct of your efforts but a necessary foundation for making bold decisions and leading your business effectively. Here's how personal development directly contributes to building the confidence you need to succeed:

1. Enhanced Knowledge and Skills: The more you learn, the more competent you become. Whether it's mastering a new technology, understanding market trends, or improving your communication skills, every bit of knowledge adds to your confidence.

2. Improved Problem-Solving Abilities: With a well-rounded set of skills

21

and a broad knowledge base, you'll be better equipped to tackle problems as they arise. This proactive approach to problem-solving can prevent issues from escalating and boost your confidence in handling unforeseen challenges.

3. Increased Self-Awareness: Personal development often involves self-reflection and mindfulness, which can lead to greater self-awareness. Understanding your strengths, weaknesses, and triggers can help you make better decisions and manage stress more effectively.

4. Stronger Leadership Qualities: Effective leadership is rooted in confidence. By investing in your personal development, you'll cultivate the qualities that make a strong leader, such as empathy, decisiveness, and the ability to inspire and motivate others.

5. Resilience and Adaptability: Developing a growth mindset and embracing continuous learning makes you more resilient to setbacks. This resilience is a key component of confidence, as it allows you to bounce back from failures and keep moving forward.

Remember, the journey of entrepreneurship is as much about personal transformation as it is about business success. Embrace the challenges, invest in your growth, and stay committed to your vision. With the right mindset and tools, you can navigate the dynamic world of entrepreneurship and achieve your dreams.

CHAPTER 3: IDENTIFYING AND VALIDATING YOUR BUSINESS IDEA

Generating Business Concepts

The first step in starting a successful business is generating viable business ideas. This process can be both exhilarating and overwhelming, as the possibilities are virtually limitless. Here are some strategies and techniques to help you brainstorm effectively and spark your creativity.

How to Brainstorm and Generate Viable Business Ideas

1. **Identify Your Interests and Passions**

- Think about what you love doing in your free time. Your hobbies and interests can often lead to great business ideas.
- **Action Step**: Make a list of your passions and interests. Consider how these can be turned into a business.

1. **Solve Problems You Encounter**

- Many successful businesses are built around solving a specific problem. Look for pain points in your daily life or industry.
- **Action Step**: Identify common frustrations or challenges you face and

brainstorm potential solutions.

1. **Leverage Your Skills and Expertise**

- Utilize your professional background, skills, and knowledge to identify business opportunities.
- **Action Step**: List your skills and expertise. Think about how these can be applied to create a business.

1. **Research Market Trends**

- Stay updated with industry trends and emerging markets. These trends can provide insights into potential business opportunities.
- **Action Step**: Read industry reports, follow relevant news, and attend conferences to identify trends.

1. **Explore Gaps in the Market**

- Look for unmet needs or underserved markets. Identifying these gaps can lead to lucrative business opportunities.
- **Action Step**: Conduct market research to identify areas where demand exceeds supply.

1. **Ask for Feedback**

- Talk to friends, family, and colleagues about your ideas. Their feedback can help refine your concepts and reveal new possibilities.
- **Action Step**: Create a survey or conduct informal interviews to gather feedback on your ideas.

1. **Think Globally**

- Consider ideas that have been successful in other regions or countries

but have yet to be available in your area.
- **Action Step**: Research international business trends and evaluate their potential in your local market.

1. **Use Idea Generation Techniques**

- Techniques such as mind mapping, brainstorming sessions, and the SCAMPER method (Substitute, Combine, Adapt, Modify, Put to another use, Eliminate, and Reverse) can help generate creative ideas.
- **Action Step**: Schedule regular brainstorming sessions and use different techniques to generate a diverse range of ideas.

Techniques to Spark Creativity

1. **Mind Mapping**

- Mind mapping is a visual brainstorming technique that helps organize and connect ideas. Start with a central concept and branch out into related ideas.
- **Action Step**: Create a mind map for each of your interests and see how they interconnect with potential business ideas.

1. **Brainstorming Sessions**

- Gather a group of people and encourage free thinking. Write down all ideas, no matter how outlandish, without judgment.
- **Action Step**: Host a brainstorming session with friends or colleagues and aim to generate as many ideas as possible.

1. **SCAMPER Technique**

- The SCAMPER technique encourages you to think about how you can improve existing products or ideas by asking specific questions.

- **Action Step**: Apply the SCAMPER technique to everyday products or services and see what new business ideas emerge.

1. **Analogies and Metaphors**

- Use analogies and metaphors to draw parallels between unrelated concepts. This can lead to innovative ideas.
- **Action Step**: Take a common problem and try to solve it using concepts from a completely different field.

1. **Reverse Thinking**

- Instead of thinking about what you can add, consider what you can take away or do differently.
- **Action Step**: Think of a successful business model and then imagine how it could be disrupted or simplified.

Checklist for Evaluating Potential Business Ideas

Market Demand

- Is there a demand for your product or service?
- Who is your target audience?

Unique Selling Proposition (USP)

- What makes your idea unique?
- How does it stand out from competitors?

Feasibility

- Can you realistically execute this idea?
- Do you have the necessary skills and resources?

Profitability

- Can this idea generate profit?
- What are the potential revenue streams?

Scalability

- Can the business grow over time?
- Are there opportunities for expansion?

Competition

- Who are your competitors?
- What are their strengths and weaknesses?

Risk Assessment

- What are the potential risks?
- How can you mitigate these risks?

Alignment with Your Goals

- Does this idea align with your personal and professional goals?
- Are you passionate about it?

Conducting SWOT Analysis

A SWOT analysis is a strategic planning tool used to identify the Strengths, Weaknesses, Opportunities, and Threats related to your business idea. It helps you understand the internal and external factors that can impact your business success.

What is a SWOT Analysis, and Why is it Important?

A SWOT analysis provides a clear framework for evaluating your business idea. It helps you:

- **Identify Strengths**: Understand what you do well and what advantages you have over competitors.
- **Recognize Weaknesses**: Be aware of areas where you need improvement or lack resources.
- **Spot Opportunities**: Identify external factors that could positively impact your business.
- **Anticipate Threats**: Recognize external challenges that could hinder your business success.

Conducting a SWOT analysis allows you to develop strategies that leverage your strengths, address your weaknesses, capitalize on opportunities, and mitigate threats.

Step-by-Step Guide on Conducting a SWOT Analysis

Identify Strengths

- **Questions to Consider**:
- What advantages does your business have?
- What unique resources do you possess?
- What do customers appreciate about your business?
- **Action Step**: List your strengths, such as skills, resources, and competitive advantages.

Recognize Weaknesses

- **Questions to Consider**:
- What areas need improvement?
- What resources do you lack?
- What do competitors do better than you?

- **Action Step**: List your weaknesses, such as limited funding, skills gaps, or operational inefficiencies.

Spot Opportunities

- **Questions to Consider**:
- What trends could benefit your business?
- Are there gaps in the market you can fill?
- What changes in technology or regulations can you leverage?
- **Action Step**: List opportunities, such as emerging markets, technological advancements, or shifts in consumer behavior.

Anticipate Threats

- **Questions to Consider**:
- What obstacles do you face?
- What are your competitors doing?
- Are there economic or regulatory changes that could impact your business?
- **Action Step**: List threats, such as new competitors, economic downturns, or changes in regulations.

Analyze and Develop Strategies

- **Action Step**: Use the insights from your SWOT analysis to develop strategies that:
- Leverage your strengths to capitalize on opportunities.
- Address and improve your weaknesses.
- Mitigate the impact of threats.

Real-Life Example of a SWOT Analysis for a Business Idea

Let's conduct a SWOT analysis for a hypothetical startup that offers eco-friendly packaging solutions.

Strengths

- Expertise in sustainable materials.
- Strong relationships with suppliers.
- Innovative product design.
- Growing consumer demand for eco-friendly products.

Weaknesses

- Limited initial funding.
- Small team with limited marketing experience.
- Higher production costs compared to traditional packaging.
- Limited brand recognition.

Opportunities

- Increasing awareness of environmental issues.
- Government incentives for sustainable businesses.
- Partnerships with eco-conscious brands.
- Expansion into international markets.

Threats

- Competition from established packaging companies.
- Fluctuations in raw material prices.
- Regulatory changes affecting production.
- Economic downturn reducing consumer spending.

Strategic Actions

- Leverage expertise and supplier relationships to create high-quality, innovative products.
- Address funding limitations by seeking investors and applying for grants.
- Reduce production costs through efficient manufacturing processes.
- Increase brand recognition through targeted marketing campaigns.
- Capitalize on opportunities by forming partnerships with eco-conscious brands and exploring international markets.
- Mitigate threats by diversifying suppliers and staying informed about regulatory changes.

Spotting Market Opportunities

Identifying gaps in the market is crucial for developing a successful business idea. By spotting opportunities, you can create products or services that meet unmet needs and stand out in the marketplace.

How to Identify Gaps in the Market
   Conduct Market Research

- Use surveys, interviews, and focus groups to gather insights from potential customers.
- Analyze industry reports and market data to identify trends and unmet needs.

Analyze Competitors

- Study your competitors to understand their strengths and weaknesses.
- Identify areas where they are not meeting customer needs or where there is room for improvement.

Leverage Customer Feedback

- Listen to customer feedback and reviews to identify common complaints or requests.
- Use this information to develop solutions that address these pain points.

Monitor Industry Trends

- Stay updated on industry trends and emerging technologies.
- Identify opportunities created by shifts in consumer behavior, regulations, or technological advancements.

Engage with Your Target Audience

- Participate in industry forums, social media groups, and online communities where your target audience engages.
- Listen to their conversations and identify recurring issues or desires.

Explore Adjacent Markets

- Look at related industries or markets for inspiration.
- Identify trends or products that could be adapted to your market.

Tools and Resources for Spotting Opportunities

Google Trends

- Use Google Trends to analyze search data and identify emerging trends and popular topics.
- This tool can help you understand what people are interested in and how their interests change over time.

Social Media Analytics

- Monitor social media platforms for trending topics, hashtags, and

conversations related to your industry.
- Use tools like Hootsuite, Sprout Social, or Brandwatch to gather insights.

Industry Reports and Publications

- Read industry reports, white papers, and publications from reputable sources.
- Organizations like IBISWorld, Statista, and Nielsen provide valuable market data and analysis.

Competitor Analysis Tools

- Use tools like SEMrush, Ahrefs, or SimilarWeb to analyze your competitors' online presence and performance.
- Identify gaps in their offerings and areas where you can differentiate.

Customer Surveys and Feedback Tools

- Use tools like SurveyMonkey, Typeform, or Google Forms to conduct surveys and gather feedback from your target audience.
- Analyze the responses to identify common themes and opportunities.

Checklist for Market Opportunity Assessment

Identify Customer Needs

- Conduct surveys and interviews to understand customer pain points and desires.
- Analyze feedback and reviews for recurring themes.

Analyze Competitors

- Identify your main competitors and analyze their strengths and weaknesses.

- Look for gaps in their offerings and areas where you can differentiate.

Evaluate Market Trends

- Stay updated on industry trends and emerging technologies.
- Identify how these trends could impact your market and create opportunities.

Assess Market Size and Growth Potential

- Research the size of your target market and its growth potential.
- Determine if there is sufficient demand to support your business idea.

Consider Regulatory and Economic Factors

- Evaluate how regulatory changes and economic conditions could impact your market.
- Identify opportunities created by these factors.

Validate Your Findings

- Test your assumptions and ideas with a small group of potential customers.
- Use their feedback to refine your concept and ensure it meets a real need.

Evaluating Ideas with the R.O.I. Concept

The Return on Investment (R.O.I.) concept is a crucial metric for evaluating the potential profitability of a business idea. It helps you determine whether the benefits of an investment outweigh the costs.

Return on Investment (R.O.I.) is a performance measure used to evaluate the efficiency of an investment. It is calculated by dividing the net profit from an investment by the initial cost of the investment and expressing the result as a percentage.

R.O.I. Formula:
R.O.I.=(Net Profit/Cost of Investment)×100

Example: If you invest $10,000 in a business idea and generate a net profit of $2,000, the R.O.I. would be:
R.O.I.=($2,000/$10,000)×100=20%

An R.O.I. of 20% means that for every dollar invested, you earned 20 cents in profit.

How to Apply R.O.I. to Evaluate Business Ideas

Estimate Initial Investment Costs

- Calculate all the costs associated with starting and running your business, including equipment, inventory, marketing, and operating expenses.
- **Action Step**: Create a detailed budget that outlines all expected expenses.

Project Revenue

- Estimate the potential revenue your business can generate based on market research, pricing strategies, and sales forecasts.
- **Action Step**: Develop a revenue model that includes different scenarios (e.g., best-case, worst-case, and most likely).

Calculate Net Profit

- Subtract your projected costs from your projected revenue to determine the net profit.

- **Action Step**: Use financial projections to calculate the expected net profit for different periods (e.g., monthly, quarterly, annually).

Determine R.O.I.

- Apply the R.O.I. formula to your net profit and initial investment cost to evaluate the potential return.
- **Action Step**: Calculate the R.O.I. for each business idea to compare their profitability.

Analyze R.O.I.

- Consider the R.O.I. in the context of other factors, such as risk, market conditions, and long-term growth potential.
- **Action Step**: Prioritize business ideas with higher R.O.I. and lower risk.

Case Study: A Successful Low-Cost Business

Business Idea: A subscription box service for eco-friendly household products.

Initial Investment:

- Product sourcing: $3,000
- Website development: $1,500
- Marketing: $2,000
- Packaging and shipping: $1,000
- Total Investment: $7,500

Projected Revenue:

- Monthly subscription fee: $30
- Initial subscribers: 200

- Monthly revenue: $6,000

Net Profit Calculation:

- Monthly expenses (product cost, shipping, marketing, etc.): $4,000
- Monthly net profit: $6,000 - $4,000 = $2,000

R.O.I. Calculation:

$$R.O.I. = (\$2,000/\$7,500) \times 100 = 26.67\%$$

With an R.O.I. of 26.67%, the subscription box service demonstrates a strong potential for profitability with a relatively low initial investment.

Identifying and validating your business idea is a critical step in your entrepreneurial journey. By generating creative business concepts, conducting thorough SWOT analyses, spotting market opportunities, and evaluating ideas using the R.O.I. concept, you can lay a solid foundation for success.

Use the techniques and checklists provided in this chapter to explore and assess your business ideas systematically. Remember, the goal is not just to find a viable idea but to identify one that aligns with your passions, leverages your strengths, and meets a genuine market need.

With careful planning, strategic thinking, and a willingness to embrace uncertainty, you can transform your business idea into a thriving venture.

CHAPTER 4: FUNDING YOUR BUSINESS

Starting a business often requires capital, and finding the right funding can be a critical step in your entrepreneurial journey. This chapter will explore various funding options, discuss how to start with minimal resources, provide principles of effective financial management and budgeting, and recommend tools and resources for financial planning.

Exploring Different Funding Sources

Securing funding is one of the most significant challenges faced by startups. The right funding can provide the necessary resources to turn your idea into a thriving business. Here are some of the primary funding options available for startups:

1. Loans

Traditional Bank Loans: Banks offer various loan products to businesses. These loans usually require a solid business plan, a good credit history, and collateral.

- **Pros**: Lower interest rates compared to other lending options; potential for large sums of capital.
- **Cons**: Lengthy application process; stringent eligibility criteria; the requirement of collateral.

SBA Loans: The Small Business Administration (SBA) offers loans to small businesses through partner lenders.

- **Pros**: Favorable terms and lower interest rates; government-backed, reducing risk for lenders.
- **Cons**: Competitive and rigorous application process; extensive documentation required.

Microloans: Smaller loans are typically offered by non-profit organizations and community lenders.

- **Pros**: Easier approval process; good for startups needing smaller amounts of capital.
- **Cons**: Higher interest rates limited loan amounts.

2. **Investments**

Angel Investors: Wealthy individuals who provide capital for startups in exchange for equity ownership or convertible debt.

- **Pros**: Access to mentorship and industry connections; no repayment obligation.
- **Cons**: Loss of equity; potential for investor involvement in business decisions.

Venture Capital: Investment firms that provide funding to startups with high growth potential in exchange for equity.

- **Pros**: Large amounts of capital, strategic support, and networking opportunities.
- **Cons**: Loss of significant equity; high expectations for rapid growth and profitability.

Crowdfunding: Raising small amounts of money from a large number of people, typically through online platforms.

- **Pros**: Access to capital without giving up equity; ability to validate business ideas and build a customer base.
- **Cons**: Intense marketing efforts are needed; funds are not guaranteed.

3. Grants

- **Government Grants**: Funds provided by federal, state, or local governments to support specific business activities or industries.
- **Pros**: No repayment required; can provide significant financial support.
- **Cons**: Highly competitive; extensive application process and strict compliance requirements.
- **Non-Profit and Foundation Grants**: Grants offered by non-profit organizations and foundations to support social enterprises or specific projects.
- **Pros**: Access to funding for mission-driven businesses; no equity loss or repayment.
- **Cons**: Limited to specific industries or causes; competitive application process.

Checklist for Choosing the Right Funding Source

Assess Your Business Needs

- Determine how much capital you need and for what purposes (e.g., startup costs, expansion, working capital).
- Identify the timeline for needing funds and the duration of financial support required.

Evaluate Your Financial Situation

- Review your credit history and financial health.
- Consider your ability to provide collateral or personal guarantees.

Understand the Terms and Conditions

- Compare interest rates, repayment terms, and any associated fees.
- Consider the implications of equity dilution and investor involvement.

Research Funding Options

- Explore various funding sources and their eligibility criteria.
- Reach out to financial advisors or mentors for recommendations.

Prepare Your Documentation

- Develop a solid business plan and financial projections.
- Gather necessary documentation, such as tax returns, credit reports, and legal documents.

Consider Non-Financial Benefits

- Look for funding sources that offer additional support, such as mentorship, industry connections, and strategic guidance.

Starting with Minimal Resources

Not all entrepreneurs have access to substantial capital at the start. Bootstrapping is a viable approach that involves starting and growing a business with limited resources. Here's how you can bootstrap your business:

1. Leverage Personal Savings

- Use your savings to fund initial expenses. This approach minimizes debt and retains full ownership of your business.

2. Reduce Initial Costs

- Start with a lean business model, focusing on essential expenses. Avoid unnecessary spending on office space, equipment, or marketing.

3. **Utilize Free or Low-Cost Tools**

- Take advantage of free or affordable tools and resources for business operations, marketing, and management.

4. **Generate Early Revenue**

- Launch a minimum viable product (MVP) to generate early revenue. Use customer feedback to improve your product or service iteratively.

5. **Reinvest Profits**

- Reinvest the profits from your business back into the company to fuel growth and expansion.

Advantages and Challenges of Bootstrapping
  Advantages:

- **Full Control**: Retain complete ownership and control over your business decisions.
- **Financial Discipline**: Encourages prudent financial management and cost control.
- **Flexibility**: Greater flexibility in adapting and pivoting business strategies.

Challenges:

- **Limited Resources**: Constraints on capital can limit growth and expansion opportunities.
- **High Personal Risk**: Personal financial risk and pressure can be signifi-

cant.

- **Slower Growth**: Growth may be slower compared to funded startups with access to larger capital.

Real-Life Examples of Successful Bootstrapped Businesses

1. **Mailchimp**: Chestnut and Kurzius started Mailchimp in 2001 as a side project to their web design agency, The Rocket Science Group. They bootstrapped the company and focused on customer needs and organic growth without seeking external venture capital funding, eventually building a successful email marketing platform without external funding.

2. **Spanx**: Sara Blakely started Spanx with **$5,000** in savings, using creativity and resourcefulness to develop her product and market it. Spanx grew into a billion-dollar company without any outside investment.

3. **GoPro**: Nick Woodman founded GoPro with his savings and a small investment from his parents. He focused on creating a high-quality product and building a strong brand, eventually turning GoPro into a global action camera leader.

Effective Financial Management and Budgeting

Financial management is crucial for the sustainability and growth of your business. Effective budgeting helps you control expenses, manage cash flow, and make informed decisions. Here are key principles and tips for financial management and budgeting:

Key Principles of Financial Management
Cash Flow Management

- Monitor cash flow regularly to ensure you have enough liquidity to cover expenses.

- Implement strategies to speed up receivables and manage payables.

Expense Control

- Track all expenses and identify areas where costs can be reduced.
- Prioritize essential expenses and avoid unnecessary spending.

Profitability Analysis

- Regularly analyze your profit margins and identify factors affecting profitability.
- Adjust pricing, cost structures, and operations to improve profitability.

Financial Planning

- Develop short-term and long-term financial plans based on realistic projections.
- Regularly review and update your financial plans to reflect changing conditions.

Debt Management

- Manage debt carefully by maintaining a healthy balance between equity and debt financing.
- Ensure timely repayment of loans to maintain good credit standing.

Tips for Creating and Sticking to a Budget

Set Clear Financial Goals

- Define your financial goals, such as revenue targets, expense limits, and profit margins.
- Align your budget with these goals to guide your financial decisions.

Categorize Expenses

- Categorize your expenses into fixed (rent, salaries) and variable (marketing, supplies) costs.
- Identify essential and non-essential expenses.

Monitor and Adjust Regularly

- Review your budget regularly to track performance against projections.
- Adjust your budget as needed based on actual performance and changing conditions.

Involve Your Team

- Involve key team members in the budgeting process to gain insights and foster accountability.
- Communicate budget goals and performance regularly.

Use Budgeting Tools

- Utilize budgeting software or spreadsheets to track and manage your budget.
- Automate financial tracking to reduce manual errors and save time.

Sample Budget Template

Category	Monthly Budget	Actual Expense	Variance
Revenue			
Sales Revenue	$10,000	$9,500	-$500
Service Revenue	$2,000	$2,200	$200
Total Revenue	$12,000	$11,700	-$300
Expenses			
Rent	$1,500	$1,500	$0
Salaries	$4,000	$4,000	$0
Marketing	$2,000	$1,800	-$200
Supplies	$500	$600	$100
Utilities	$300	$320	$20
Miscellaneous	$200	$150	-$50
Total Expenses	$8,500	$8,370	-$130
Net Profit	$3,500	$3,330	-$170

Tools and Resources for Financial Planning

Effective financial planning involves using the right tools and resources to manage your business finances efficiently. Here are some recommended tools and resources:

Financial Planning Tools

Accounting Software

- **QuickBooks**: Popular accounting software for small businesses, offering features like invoicing, expense tracking, and financial reporting.
- **Xero**: Cloud-based accounting software with real-time financial data and integration with various business apps.
- **FreshBooks**: Easy-to-use accounting software designed for small business owners, focusing on invoicing and expense management.

Budgeting Tools

- **PlanGuru**: Budgeting and forecasting software that helps businesses create detailed financial plans and analyze performance.
- **LivePlan**: Business planning software that includes budgeting, forecasting, and performance tracking features.
- **You Need A Budget (YNAB)**: Personal budgeting software that can also be used for small business financial management.

Financial Analysis Tools

- **Pulse**: Cash flow management tool that helps businesses track income, expenses, and cash flow projections.
- **Fathom**: Financial analysis and reporting tool that provides insights into business performance and financial health.
- **Sage Intacct**: Comprehensive financial management software with advanced reporting and analysis capabilities.

Resources for Financial Planning

- Online Courses and Tutorials
- Books
- Mentorship and Advisory Services

Funding your business is a critical step in turning your entrepreneurial vision into reality. By exploring different funding sources, bootstrapping with minimal resources, and practicing effective financial management and budgeting, you can secure the capital needed to grow your business sustainably.

Remember to utilize financial planning tools and resources to manage your finances efficiently. Whether you choose to seek external funding or bootstrap your business, maintaining a clear understanding of your financial situation and planning strategically will help you navigate the challenges of entrepreneurship and achieve long-term success.

By following the guidelines and strategies outlined in this chapter, you can make informed decisions about funding your business and managing your finances effectively. Embrace the journey with confidence, and you'll be well-equipped to build a successful and financially sound business.

CHAPTER 5: DEVELOPING YOUR BUSINESS PLAN

A well-crafted business plan is the foundation of any successful venture. It serves as a roadmap for your business, guiding you through the early stages of development and providing a clear path for growth. In this chapter, we will explore the essential elements of a business plan, how to write an engaging executive summary, conduct market research, structure your management team, and more. By the end of this chapter, you will have the knowledge and tools to create a comprehensive business plan that sets your business up for success.

Essential Elements of a Business Plan

What Are the Critical Components of a Business Plan?

A business plan is composed of several key components, each serving a specific purpose. These elements collectively provide a comprehensive overview of your business, its goals, and how you plan to achieve them. The critical components of a business plan include:

1. **Executive Summary**: A brief overview of your business, including your mission statement, products or services, and basic information about the company's leadership, employees, and location. It should also include financial information and high-level growth plans.
2. **Company Description**: Detailed information about your company,

including the nature of your business, the marketplace needs that you intend to meet, and the unique qualities that give your business a competitive edge.

3. **Market Research**: Analysis of your industry, market size, expected growth, and your target market's demographics, needs, and buying behavior. This section should also include an analysis of your competitors and how you plan to differentiate your business.

4. **Organization and Management**: An overview of your business's organizational structure, including details about the ownership, management team, and board of directors (if applicable).

5. **Products or Services**: A detailed description of your products or services, including information on the benefits and competitive advantages they offer.

6. **Marketing and Sales Strategy**: Your plan for reaching and attracting your target market, including your marketing strategy, sales tactics, and how you plan to retain customers.

7. **Operations Plan**: An outline of your business's operational requirements, including location, facilities, equipment, and processes for producing your product or service.

8. **Financial Projections**: Detailed financial forecasts, including income statements, cash flow statements, and balance sheets for the next three to five years. This section should also include a break-even analysis and information about your funding requirements.

9. **Appendices**: Any additional information that supports your business plan, such as resumes, permits, lease agreements, legal documentation, and other pertinent documents.

How Do These Elements Contribute to Business Success?

Each component of a business plan plays a vital role in the success of your business:

- **Executive Summary**: Captures the attention of investors and stakeholders, providing a concise and compelling overview of your business.

- **Company Description**: Clearly articulate your business's purpose, vision, and unique value proposition, helping stakeholders understand your goals.
- **Market Research**: Provides critical insights into your industry and target market, enabling you to make informed strategic decisions.
- **Organization and Management**: Demonstrates your leadership and management capabilities, instilling confidence in investors and stakeholders.
- **Products or Services**: Highlights the benefits and competitive advantages of your offerings, attracting customers and investors.
- **Marketing and Sales Strategy**: Outlines how you will reach and retain customers, driving sales and growth.
- **Operations Plan**: Ensures you have the necessary infrastructure and processes in place to deliver your products or services efficiently.
- **Financial Projections**: Provides a clear financial roadmap, helping you secure funding and manage your business's finances effectively.
- **Appendices**: Offers additional documentation that supports your business plan and provides further validation of your business's viability.

Checklist for Business Plan Components

Executive Summary

- Mission statement
- Overview of products/services
- Leadership and team
- Financial highlights
- Growth plans

Company Description

- Business name and location
- Nature of business

- Market needs addressed
- Competitive advantages

Market Research

- Industry analysis
- Market size and growth
- Target market demographics
- Competitive analysis

Organization and Management

- Ownership structure
- Management team
- Board of directors

Products or Services

- Product/service description
- Benefits and advantages
- Product lifecycle
- Intellectual property

Marketing and Sales Strategy

- Marketing strategy
- Sales tactics
- Customer retention plans

Operations Plan

- Operational requirements
- Location and Facilities

- Production process
- Supply chain management

Financial Projections

- Income statements
- Cash flow statements
- Balance sheets
- Break-even analysis
- Funding requirements

Appendices

- Resumes
- Permits and licenses
- Legal documents
- Other supporting documents

Writing an Engaging Executive Summary

How to Craft a Compelling Executive Summary:

The executive summary is arguably the most crucial part of your business plan. It provides a snapshot of your business and is often the first section investors and stakeholders read. A compelling executive summary should be concise, engaging, and informative. Here's how to craft one:

1. **Start with a Hook**: Begin with a strong opening statement that captures the reader's attention. This could be a compelling fact, a market opportunity, or a powerful quote.
2. **Describe Your Business**: Provide a brief overview of your business, including its name, location, and the products or services you offer.
3. **State Your Mission**: Clearly articulate your business's mission statement and core values.

4. **Highlight Key Information**: Summarize the most critical information from each section of your business plan, such as market research insights, unique value propositions, and financial highlights.

5. **Include Financial Projections**: Offer a snapshot of your financial projections, including revenue, expenses, and profit margins.

6. **Outline Your Growth Strategy**: Briefly describe your growth plans and how you intend to achieve them.

7. **Keep It Concise**: Aim for one to two pages. The executive summary should be a high-level overview, not an exhaustive description.

What Key Information Should It Include?

A strong executive summary should include the following key information:

1. **Business Overview**: A brief description of your business, including its name, location, and the products or services offered.

2. **Mission Statement**: A clear and concise statement of your business's mission and core values.

3. **Market Opportunity**: An overview of the market opportunity, including key market research findings and target audience insights.

4. **Unique Value Proposition**: A summary of what sets your business apart from competitors and the unique benefits of your products or services.

5. **Financial Highlights**: Key financial projections, including revenue, expenses, and profit margins.

6. **Growth Strategy**: A brief description of your growth plans and the strategies you will use to achieve them.

7. **Management Team**: An introduction to your management team and their qualifications.

8. **Funding Requirements**: If applicable, a summary of your funding needs and how the funds will be used.

Example of a Strong Executive Summary

Executive Summary: ABC Organic Skincare

Business Overview: ABC Organic Skincare is a premium skincare company based in San Francisco, California. We specialize in creating high-quality, organic skincare products that cater to health-conscious consumers seeking natural and effective skincare solutions.

Mission Statement: Our mission is to revolutionize the skincare industry by offering products that are not only effective but also environmentally sustainable. We are committed to promoting skin health and environmental responsibility through our innovative product line.

Market Opportunity: The global organic skincare market is projected to grow at a CAGR of 8.5% over the next five years, reaching $25 billion by 2025. With increasing consumer awareness about the harmful effects of synthetic chemicals, there is a growing demand for natural and organic skincare products. Our target market includes health-conscious individuals aged 25-45 who prioritize quality and sustainability in their skincare choices.

Unique Value Proposition: ABC Organic Skincare stands out due to our use of certified organic ingredients, eco-friendly packaging, and cruelty-free testing. A team of dermatologists and herbalists formulate our products to ensure efficacy and safety. We are dedicated to transparency, and each product comes with a detailed ingredient list and sourcing information.

Financial highlights: In our first year of operation, we project revenue of **$500,000**, with a net profit margin of 20%. By year three, we anticipate revenue of **$2 million**, driven by product line expansion and increased market penetration.

Growth Strategy: We plan to achieve our growth goals through a combination of online and offline marketing strategies, including social media campaigns, influencer partnerships, and participation in industry trade shows. We will also expand our product line to include new skincare categories and enter international markets.

Management Team: Our management team comprises industry experts with extensive experience in skincare formulation, marketing, and business development. Jane Doe, our CEO, has over 15 years of experience in the skincare industry, while John Smith, our COO, has a background in supply chain management and operations.

Funding Requirements: We are seeking $250,000 in funding to support our product development, marketing efforts, and operational expansion. These funds will enable us to scale our business and achieve our growth objectives.

Crafting a Detailed Company Description

What Should Be Included in a Company Description?

The company description section of your business plan provides a comprehensive overview of your business, including its history, vision, mission, and the market needs it addresses. Here's what to include:

1. **Business Name and Location**: Provide the official name of your business and its location.
2. **Nature of Business**: Describe the nature of your business, including the products or services you offer.
3. **Market Needs**: Explain the specific market needs your business addresses and how your products or services fulfill these needs.
4. **Business History**: If applicable, provide a brief history of your business, including key milestones and achievements.
5. **Vision and Mission**: Clearly state your business's vision and mission. The vision statement outlines your long-term goals, while the mission statement defines your purpose and core values.
6. **Business Objectives**: Outline your short-term and long-term business objectives and how you plan to achieve them.
7. **Legal Structure**: Specify the legal structure of your business (e.g., sole proprietorship, partnership, corporation).

How Can It Effectively Convey the Business's Vision and Mission?

To effectively convey your business's vision and mission, ensure that these statements are clear, concise, and inspiring. Your vision statement should paint a picture of what you aspire to achieve in the future, while your mission statement should communicate your purpose and core values. Here are some tips:

Vision Statement

- Be aspirational and forward-looking.
- Reflect on your long-term goals and aspirations.
- Keep it concise and memorable.

Mission Statement

- Clearly define your business's purpose and core values.
- Focus on what you do and why you do it.
- Make it meaningful and inspiring to both employees and customers.

Company Description Template

Business Name: [Your Business Name]**Location**: [Your Business Location]

Nature of Business[Briefly describe the nature of your business, including the products or services you offer.]

Market Needs[Explain the specific market needs your business addresses and how your products or services fulfill these needs.]

Business History[Provide a brief history of your business, including key milestones and achievements, if applicable.]

Vision Statement[Clearly state your business's vision, outlining your long-term goals and aspirations.]

Mission Statement[Define your business's purpose and core values, focusing on what you do and why you do it.]

Business Objectives[Outline your short-term and long-term business objectives and how you plan to achieve them.]

Legal Structure[Specify the legal structure of your business (e.g., sole proprietorship, partnership, corporation).]

Conducting Market Research

Conducting thorough market research is essential for understanding your industry, market size, target audience, and competition. Here are some methods you can use:

Primary Research: Gather firsthand information directly from your target market through surveys, interviews, focus groups, and observations.

- **Surveys**: Distribute questionnaires to collect data on customer preferences, behaviors, and opinions.
- **Interviews**: Conduct one-on-one interviews with potential customers, industry experts, and stakeholders to gain deeper insights.
- **Focus Groups**: Organize group discussions with a small number of participants to explore their attitudes and perceptions.
- **Observations**: Observe customer behavior in real-world settings to gather insights into their needs and preferences.

Secondary Research: Use existing data and research from credible sources to gather information about your industry and market.

- **Industry Reports**: Access reports from market research firms, trade associations, and government agencies.
- **Academic Research**: Review studies and publications from universities and research institutions.
- **Competitor Analysis**: Analyze competitors' websites, marketing materials, and financial reports to understand their strategies and performance.

Data Analysis: Analyze the data you collect to identify trends, patterns, and insights that can inform your business strategy.

- **Quantitative Analysis**: Use statistical methods to analyze numerical data and identify trends.

- **Qualitative Analysis**: Interpret non-numerical data, such as interview transcripts and survey responses, to gain deeper insights.

Market research provides critical insights that can inform your business strategy in several ways:

1. **Understanding Customer Needs**: Identify the needs, preferences, and behaviors of your target market, allowing you to tailor your products and services to meet their demands.
2. **Identifying Market Opportunities**: Discover gaps in the market and emerging trends that present opportunities for growth and innovation.
3. **Assessing Market Size and Growth**: Estimate the size of your target market and its growth potential, helping you make informed decisions about market entry and expansion.
4. **Analyzing Competitors**: Gain insights into your competitors' strengths, weaknesses, and strategies, enabling you to differentiate your business and identify areas for improvement.
5. **Informing Marketing and Sales Strategies**: Use market research to develop effective marketing and sales strategies that resonate with your target audience and drive customer acquisition and retention.
6. **Mitigating Risks**: Identify potential risks and challenges in your industry, allowing you to develop strategies to mitigate them and make informed decisions.

Checklist for Conducting Market Research
Define Research Objectives

- Identify the specific questions you want to answer through your market research.
- Set clear objectives to guide your research efforts.

Choose Research Methods

59

- Decide whether to use primary research, secondary research, or a combination of both.
- Select appropriate research methods (surveys, interviews, focus groups).

Collect Data

- Gather data from credible sources using your chosen research methods.
- Ensure data collection is systematic and unbiased.

Analyze Data

- Use quantitative and qualitative analysis techniques to interpret the data.
- Identify trends, patterns, and insights that inform your business strategy.

Draw Conclusions

- Summarize your findings and draw conclusions based on the data analysis.
- Make informed decisions and develop strategies based on your research.

Present Findings

- Organize your findings into a clear and concise report.
- Use visuals (charts, graphs, tables) to present data effectively.

Structuring Your Management Team

Outlining the management structure in your business plan is important for several reasons:

1. **Demonstrates Leadership**: Showcases the qualifications and experience of your management team, instilling confidence in investors and stakeholders.

2. **Clarifies Roles and Responsibilities**: Clearly defines the roles and responsibilities of each team member, ensuring accountability and efficient decision-making.

3. **Supports Strategic Planning**: Helps you identify any gaps in your team and plan for future hiring needs.

4. **Enhances Communication**: Facilitates effective communication and collaboration within the team by establishing a clear organizational hierarchy.

How Can Entrepreneurs Build a Strong Management Team?

Building a strong management team involves selecting individuals with the right skills, experience, and qualities to lead your business. Here are some steps to help you build a strong team:

1. **Identify Key Roles**: Determine the key roles and responsibilities needed to run your business effectively. Common roles include CEO, COO, CFO, CMO, and department heads.

2. **Define Qualifications**: Outline the qualifications, skills, and experience required for each role. Consider both technical expertise and leadership qualities.

3. **Recruit and Hire**: Use a thorough recruitment process to identify and hire the best candidates for each role. Consider using professional networks, job boards, and recruitment agencies.

4. **Foster a Positive Culture**: Create a positive and inclusive work environment that encourages collaboration, innovation, and continuous improvement.

5. **Provide Training and Development**: Invest in training and development programs to help your team members enhance their skills and grow professionally.

6. **Encourage Open Communication**: Promote open and transparent communication within the team to build trust and facilitate effective decision-making.

Sample Management Team Structure

CEO (Chief Executive Officer): Responsible for overall strategic direction and management of the company.

COO (Chief Operating Officer): Oversees daily operations and ensures efficient business processes.

CFO (Chief Financial Officer): Manages financial planning, budgeting, and financial reporting.

CMO (Chief Marketing Officer): Leads marketing and sales efforts, including branding, advertising, and customer acquisition.

CTO (Chief Technology Officer): Oversees technology strategy, development, and implementation.

HR Director: Manages human resources functions, including recruitment, training, and employee relations.

Operations Manager: Ensures smooth and efficient production and delivery of products or services.

Sales Manager: Leads the sales team and develops strategies to drive revenue growth.

Customer Service Manager: Oversees customer support and ensures high levels of customer satisfaction.

Defining Your Products and Services

When describing your products or services, it is essential to provide a clear and detailed explanation of what you offer and how it benefits your customers. Here's what to include:

1. **Product/Service Description**: Provide a detailed description of your products or services, including their features, functions, and specifications.
2. **Benefits and Advantages**: Highlight the unique benefits and competitive advantages of your products or services. Explain how they address customer needs and solve problems.
3. **Target Market**: Identify the specific customer segments that will benefit

from your products or services.

4. **Product Lifecycle**: Describe the lifecycle of your products, including development, launch, growth, maturity, and decline stages.

5. **Intellectual Property**: If applicable, mention any patents, trademarks, or copyrights associated with your products or services.

What Details Are Essential to Include?

To provide a comprehensive description of your products or services, include the following details:

1. **Product/Service Name**: Clearly state the name of your product or service.

2. **Features and Specifications**: List the key features and technical specifications of your product or service.

3. **Benefits and Advantages**: Explain the benefits and advantages, emphasizing how they meet customer needs and provide value.

4. **Pricing**: Provide pricing information, including any pricing models or tiers.

5. **Distribution Channels**: Describe how your products or services will be distributed to customers (e.g., online, retail, direct sales).

6. **Customer Support**: Outline the customer support and after-sales services you will provide.

Template for Product and Service Descriptions

Product/Service Name: [Name of Product/Service]

Description: [Provide a detailed description of your product or service, including its features, functions, and specifications.]

Benefits and Advantages: [Highlight the unique benefits and competitive advantages of your product or service.]

Target Market: [Identify the specific customer segments that will benefit from your product or service.]

Product Lifecycle: [Describe the lifecycle of your product, including development, launch, growth, maturity, and decline stages.]

Intellectual Property: [Mention any patents, trademarks, or copyrights associated with your product or service, if applicable.]

Pricing: [Provide pricing information, including any pricing models or tiers.]

Distribution Channels: [Describe how your product or service will be distributed to customers.]

Customer Support: [Outline the customer support and after-sales services you will provide.]

Segmenting Your Customers

Customer segmentation is the process of dividing a broad target market into smaller, more manageable groups of customers with similar characteristics, needs, and behaviors. Segmentation is important because it allows businesses to:

1. **Tailor Marketing Efforts**: Develop targeted marketing campaigns that resonate with specific customer segments, increasing the effectiveness of your marketing efforts.
2. **Personalize Customer Experience**: Provide personalized products, services, and experiences that meet the unique needs of each customer segment.
3. **Improve Customer Retention**: Enhance customer satisfaction and loyalty by addressing the specific needs and preferences of different segments.
4. **Optimize Resources**: Allocate marketing and sales resources more efficiently by focusing on the most profitable and high-potential customer segments.

How Can Businesses Effectively Segment Their Target Market?

To effectively segment your target market, follow these steps:

Identify Segmentation Criteria: Choose criteria for segmentation based on demographics, psychographics, behavior, and geography.

- **Demographics**: Age, gender, income, education, occupation.
- **Psychographics**: Lifestyle, values, interests, attitudes.
- **Behavior**: Purchase behavior, usage patterns, brand loyalty.
- **Geography**: Location, region, climate.

Collect Data: Gather data on your target market using surveys, interviews, focus groups, and secondary research.

Analyze Data: Analyze the data to identify patterns and similarities among customers. Group customers into distinct segments based on the chosen criteria.

Develop Customer Profiles: Create detailed profiles for each customer segment, including information about their needs, preferences, and behaviors.

Evaluate Segments: Assess the attractiveness and potential profitability of each segment. Consider factors such as market size, growth potential, and competitive landscape.

Select Target Segments: Choose the segments that align best with your business goals and capabilities.

Developing a Marketing and Sales Strategy

A comprehensive marketing plan outlines how you will reach and attract your target market, build brand awareness, and drive sales. Here's what to include:

1. **Market Analysis**: Summarize your market research findings, including industry trends, target market demographics, and competitive analysis.
2. **Marketing Goals**: Define your marketing objectives, such as increasing brand awareness, generating leads, or boosting sales.
3. **Target Market**: Identify your target market segments and develop customer profiles for each segment.

4. **Unique Selling Proposition (USP)**: Highlight what sets your products or services apart from competitors and why customers should choose your brand.

5. **Marketing Strategies**: Outline the strategies you will use to achieve your marketing goals. This may include digital marketing, content marketing, social media marketing, influencer partnerships, email marketing, and traditional advertising.

6. **Marketing Budget**: Allocate a budget for your marketing activities and outline how the funds will be spent.

7. **Marketing Timeline**: Create a timeline for your marketing activities, including key milestones and deadlines.

8. **Metrics and Evaluation**: Define the key performance indicators (KPIs) you will use to measure the success of your marketing efforts. Include a plan for evaluating and adjusting your strategies based on performance data.

How Can You Develop a Sales Strategy That Works?

Developing a sales strategy involves creating a plan to generate leads, convert prospects into customers, and retain existing customers. Here's how to develop an effective sales strategy:

1. **Define Sales Goals**: Set clear, measurable sales goals that align with your overall business objectives. These goals should be specific, achievable, and time-bound.

2. **Identify Target Customers**: Use your customer segmentation data to identify the specific customer segments you will target with your sales efforts.

3. **Develop a Sales Process**: Create a step-by-step sales process that outlines how you will generate leads, qualify prospects, present your product or service, handle objections, close sales, and follow up with customers.

4. **Choose Sales Channels**: Determine the sales channels you will use to reach your target customers. This may include direct sales, online sales,

retail sales, and partnerships.

5. **Create Sales Materials**: Develop sales materials that support your sales efforts, such as brochures, presentations, product demos, and case studies.

6. **Train Your Sales Team**: Provide training and resources to ensure your sales team is knowledgeable, skilled, and motivated.

7. **Implement Sales Tools**: Use sales tools and software to streamline your sales process, manage leads, and track performance.

8. **Monitor and Adjust**: Regularly review your sales performance data and adjust your strategy as needed to improve results.

Sample Marketing and Sales Plan

Market Analysis

- The organic skincare market is projected to grow at a CAGR of 8.5% over the next five years.
- Target market: Health-conscious individuals aged 25-45 who prioritize quality and sustainability in skincare products.
- Competitors: Established brands like Burt's Bees, Dr. Bronner's, and smaller indie brands.

Marketing Goals

- Increase brand awareness by 50% within the first year.
- Generate 10,000 leads and achieve a 5% conversion rate within six months.
- Boost online sales by 30% in the first year.

Target Market

- Segment 1: Eco-conscious millennials seeking natural skincare solutions.
- Segment 2: Health-focused professionals aged 35-45 with disposable income.

Unique Selling Proposition (USP)

- Our products are made from certified organic ingredients, packaged in eco-friendly materials, and formulated by dermatologists and herbalists.

Marketing Strategies

- **Digital Marketing**: Launch a content marketing campaign focused on skincare tips, ingredient benefits, and sustainable beauty practices.
- **Social Media Marketing**: Partner with eco-conscious influencers to promote our products on Instagram and YouTube.
- **Email Marketing**: Develop a lead magnet (e.g., a free e-book on organic skincare) to build our email list and nurture leads through a series of automated emails.
- **Traditional Advertising**: Place ads in health and wellness magazines and participate in industry trade shows.

Marketing Budget

- Digital Marketing: $15,000
- Social Media Marketing: $10,000
- Email Marketing: $5,000
- Traditional Advertising: $10,000
- Total: $40,000

Marketing Timeline

- Q1: Launch website and social media channels, develop a content marketing plan, and create a lead magnet.
- Q2: Start influencer partnerships, launch an email marketing campaign, and place traditional ads.
- Q3: Participate in industry trade shows and evaluate marketing performance.

- Q4: Adjust strategies based on performance data and plan for the following year.

Metrics and Evaluation

- Website traffic: Monitor monthly visits and page views.
- Lead generation: Track the number of leads generated through various channels.
- Conversion rate: Measure the percentage of leads that convert to customers.
- Sales revenue: Analyze monthly sales data to assess growth.

Planning Operations and Logistics

What Are the Key Considerations for Planning Operations?

Planning operations involves outlining the processes, resources, and infrastructure needed to produce and deliver your products or services. Key considerations include:

1. **Location and Facilities**: Choose a location that meets your operational needs and budget. Consider factors such as proximity to suppliers, transportation access, and local regulations.
2. **Production Process**: Define the steps involved in producing your products or services. Identify the necessary equipment, materials, and labor.
3. **Supply Chain Management**: Develop a supply chain strategy that ensures timely delivery of raw materials and components. Build relationships with reliable suppliers and establish inventory management practices.
4. **Quality Control**: Implement quality control measures to ensure your products or services meet the desired standards. Develop procedures for testing, inspection, and continuous improvement.
5. **Logistics and Distribution**: Plan the logistics and distribution of your

products, including warehousing, transportation, and delivery. Choose efficient and cost-effective methods to reach your customers.

How Can Logistics Be Efficiently Managed?

Efficient logistics management is essential for ensuring timely delivery, reducing costs, and maintaining customer satisfaction. Here are some tips for managing logistics efficiently:

1. **Streamline Processes**: Simplify and automate logistics processes to reduce errors and improve efficiency. Use technology to track inventory, shipments, and deliveries.
2. **Optimize Inventory Management**: Implement inventory management practices that balance stock levels and reduce excess inventory. Use just-in-time (JIT) inventory systems to minimize storage costs.
3. **Choose Reliable Partners**: Build relationships with reliable suppliers, carriers, and logistics providers. Negotiate favorable terms and establish clear communication channels.
4. **Monitor Performance**: Regularly monitor key performance indicators (KPIs) such as delivery times, order accuracy, and transportation costs. Use data to identify areas for improvement.
5. **Implement Technology**: Use logistics management software to track shipments, manage inventory, and optimize routes. Consider using warehouse management systems (WMS) and transportation management systems (TMS) to enhance efficiency.

Checklist for Operations Planning

1. **Location and Facilities**

- Choose a suitable location.
- Plan the layout of facilities.
- Ensure compliance with local regulations.

70

1. **Production Process**

   - Define production steps.
   - Identify necessary equipment and materials.
   - Plan labor requirements.

1. **Supply Chain Management**

   - Develop a supply chain strategy.
   - Build relationships with suppliers.
   - Implement inventory management practices.

1. **Quality Control**

   - Develop quality control procedures.
   - Implement testing and inspection processes.
   - Establish continuous improvement practices.

1. **Logistics and Distribution**

   - Plan logistics and distribution processes.
   - Choose warehousing and transportation methods.
   - Implement logistics management technology.

Creating Financial Projections

How Can Readers Develop Realistic Financial Projections?

Developing realistic financial projections involves creating detailed forecasts of your business's financial performance. Here's how to create accurate financial projections:

1. **Gather Historical Data**: If you have an existing business, use historical financial data as a baseline for your projections. Analyze trends in

revenue, expenses, and profitability.

2. **Estimate Revenue**: Forecast your sales revenue based on market re-search, customer demand, pricing strategies, and sales channels. Consider factors such as seasonality, market trends, and competitive landscape.

3. **Project Expenses**: Estimate your operating expenses, including fixed costs (rent, salaries) and variable costs (materials, marketing). Include one-time startup costs and ongoing expenses.

4. **Create Financial Statements**: Develop key financial statements, including income statements, cash flow statements, and balance sheets. Use these statements to forecast your financial performance over the next three to five years.

5. **Conduct Break-Even Analysis**: Determine the break-even point at which your business will cover its costs and start generating profit. This analysis helps you understand the sales volume needed to achieve profitability.

6. **Validate Assumptions**: Ensure your projections are based on realistic and validated assumptions. Seek input from industry experts, mentors, and financial advisors.

Tools and Templates for Financial Projections

1. **Spreadsheet Software**: Use spreadsheet software like Microsoft Excel or Google Sheets to create financial projections. These tools offer templates and functions for calculating revenue, expenses, and financial statements.

2. **Financial Planning Software**: Consider using financial planning software like QuickBooks, Xero, or LivePlan. These tools offer features for budgeting, forecasting, and financial analysis.

3. **Financial Advisors**: Consult with financial advisors or accountants to validate your projections and provide expert insights.

Sample Financial Projection Template

Income Statement

Category	Year 1	Year 2	Year 3
Revenue			
Sales Revenue	$100,000	$150,000	$200,000
Service Revenue	$20,000	$30,000	$40,000
Total Revenue	$120,000	$180,000	$240,000
Expenses			
Rent	$12,000	$12,000	$12,000
Salaries	$40,000	$50,000	$60,000
Marketing	$10,000	$15,000	$20,000
Supplies	$5,000	$7,000	$9,000
Utilities	$3,000	$3,500	$4,000
Miscellaneous	$2,000	$2,500	$3,000
Total Expenses	$72,000	$90,000	$108,000
Net Profit	$48,000	$90,000	$132,000

Cash Flow Statement

Category	Year 1	Year 2	Year 3
Cash Inflows			
Sales Revenue	$100,000	$150,000	$200,000
Service Revenue	$20,000	$30,000	$40,000
Total Inflows	$120,000	$180,000	$240,000
Cash Outflows			
Rent	$12,000	$12,000	$12,000
Salaries	$40,000	$50,000	$60,000
Marketing	$10,000	$15,000	$20,000
Supplies	$5,000	$7,000	$9,000
Utilities	$3,000	$3,500	$4,000
Miscellaneous	$2,000	$2,500	$3,000
Total Outflows	$72,000	$90,000	$108,000
Net Cash Flow	$48,000	$90,000	$132,000

Balance Sheet

Category	Year 1	Year 2	Year 3
Assets			
Cash	$20,000	$25,000	$30,000
Accounts Receivable	$15,000	$20,000	$25,000
Inventory	$10,000	$12,000	$15,000
Equipment	$5,000	$7,000	$9,000
Total Assets	$50,000	$64,000	$79,000
Liabilities			
Accounts Payable	$10,000	$12,000	$15,000
Loans	$5,000	$7,000	$9,000
Total Liabilities	$15,000	$19,000	$24,000
Equity			
Owner's Equity	$35,000	$45,000	$55,000
Total Equity	$35,000	$45,000	$55,000
Total Liabilities and Equity	$50,000	$64,000	$79,000

Case Study: A Detailed Business Plan Example

Business Plan for XYZ Tech Solutions

Executive Summary

XYZ Tech Solutions is an innovative technology company based in New York City. We specialize in developing cutting-edge software solutions for small and medium-sized enterprises (SMEs) to enhance their operational efficiency and drive growth. Our mission is to empower businesses with affordable and scalable technology solutions that deliver measurable results.

Company Description

Business Name: XYZ Tech Solutions**Location**: New York City, NY

Nature of Business: XYZ Tech Solutions develops software applications tailored to the needs of SMEs, including project management tools, customer relationship management (CRM) systems, and inventory management software.

Market Needs: SMEs often struggle with outdated and inefficient software systems that hinder their productivity and growth. Our solutions address these pain points by offering user-friendly, customizable, and cost-effective software.

Business History: Founded in 2020 by Jane Doe, XYZ Tech Solutions has quickly gained recognition for its innovative products and exceptional customer service. Key milestones include the launch of our flagship product, ProjectPro, and securing our first 100 customers within six months.

Vision Statement: To be the leading provider of innovative software solutions that empower SMEs to achieve their full potential.

Mission Statement: Our mission is to deliver affordable, scalable, and user-friendly software solutions that enhance the operational efficiency of SMEs, enabling them to grow and succeed in a competitive market.

Business Objectives

- Achieve **$1 million** in revenue by the end of year two.
- Expand our product line to include at least three new software applications within the next 18 months.
- Establish a presence in five international markets within three years.

Legal Structure: XYZ Tech Solutions is registered as a Limited Liability Company (LLC).

Market Research

Industry Analysis: The global business software market is projected to grow at a CAGR of 10% over the next five years, driven by the increasing adoption of digital solutions by SMEs.

Target Market: Our target market includes SMEs in various industries, such as retail, manufacturing, and professional services, with annual revenues between $1 million and $50 million.

Competitive Analysis: Our main competitors include established software providers like Salesforce, Zoho, and Freshworks. We differentiate ourselves by offering customizable and affordable solutions tailored specifically to the needs of SMEs.

Customer Segmentation

- Segment 1: Small retail businesses seeking inventory management solutions.
- Segment 2: Professional services firms needing project management and CRM tools.
- Segment 3: Manufacturing companies looking for integrated software to streamline operations.

Organization and Management

CEO (Chief Executive Officer): Jane Doe - Over 15 years of experience in the software industry, specializing in product development and business strategy.

COO (Chief Operating Officer): John Smith - Background in operations management and supply chain logistics, with a track record of improving efficiency and reducing costs.

CFO (Chief Financial Officer): Mary Johnson - Expertise in financial planning, budgeting, and financial analysis, with experience in both startups and established companies.

CTO (Chief Technology Officer): David Brown - Over 10 years of experience in software development and technology innovation, with a focus on creating scalable solutions.

Products and Services

Product/Service Name: ProjectPro

Description: ProjectPro is a comprehensive project management tool designed for SMEs. It offers features such as task tracking, time management, collaboration tools, and reporting.

Benefits and Advantages: ProjectPro improves productivity, enhances collaboration, and provides real-time insights into project performance, helping businesses complete projects on time and within budget.

Target Market: Professional services firms, including marketing agencies, consulting firms, and legal practices.

Product Lifecycle: ProjectPro is in the growth stage, with continuous updates and improvements based on customer feedback.

Intellectual Property: ProjectPro is protected by a registered trademark and several software patents.

Pricing: Subscription-based pricing model with tiers starting at $20 per user per month.

Distribution Channels: These are available online through our website and partner platforms.

Customer Support: 24/7 customer support via phone, email, and live chat.

Marketing and Sales Strategy

Marketing Goals

- Increase brand awareness by 50% within the first year.
- Generate 5,000 qualified leads and achieve a 10% conversion rate within six months.

Marketing Strategies

- **Content Marketing**: Develop and distribute high-quality content, including blog posts, whitepapers, and case studies, to attract and engage our target audience.
- **Social Media Marketing**: Leverage social media platforms to build a community of followers, share valuable content, and engage with potential customers.
- **Email Marketing**: Create targeted email campaigns to nurture leads, provide product updates, and offer promotions.
- **Paid Advertising**: Use Google Ads and LinkedIn Ads to drive traffic to our website and generate leads.
- **Public Relations**: Gain media coverage and build relationships with industry influencers to enhance our brand credibility.

Sales Strategy

- **Sales Process**: Implement a structured sales process, including lead generation, qualification, product demos, proposal submission, and closing deals.
- **Sales Channels**: Focus on direct sales through our website and sales team, with plans to develop partnerships with industry associations and resellers.
- **Sales Materials**: Develop product brochures, presentations, case studies, and demo videos to support our sales efforts.
- **Sales Training**: Provide ongoing training and development programs for

our sales team to ensure they are knowledgeable and skilled.

Operations and Logistics
Location and Facilities

- Headquartered in New York City, with plans to open satellite offices in key international markets.

Production Process

- Software development follows an agile methodology, with iterative cycles of planning, development, testing, and deployment.
- Continuous integration and continuous deployment (CI/CD) practices are used to ensure rapid and reliable delivery of software updates.

Supply Chain Management

- Collaborate with reliable technology partners for hosting, security, and support services.
- Implement inventory management practices for hardware and software resources.

Quality Control

- Conduct regular testing and quality assurance to ensure software reliability and performance.
- Gather user feedback and implement continuous improvement processes.

Logistics and Distribution

- Software is distributed digitally via our website and partner platforms.
- Customer onboarding and training are conducted online through webinars and video tutorials.

Financial Projections
XYZ Tech Solutions Income Statement

Category	Year 1	Year 2	Year 3
Revenue			
Software Sales	$500,000	$1,000,000	$2,000,000
Service Revenue	$100,000	$200,000	$300,000
Total Revenue	$600,000	$1,200,000	$2,300,000
Expenses			
Rent	$50,000	$60,000	$70,000
Salaries	$200,000	$250,000	$300,000
Marketing	$100,000	$150,000	$200,000
Development	$100,000	$120,000	$140,000
Utilities	$10,000	$12,000	$14,000
Miscellaneous	$5,000	$6,000	$7,000
Total Expenses	$465,000	$598,000	$731,000
Net Profit	$135,000	$602,000	$1,569,000

XYZ Tech Solutions Cash Flow Statement

Category	Year 1	Year 2	Year 3
Cash Inflows			
Software Sales	$500,000	$1,000,000	$2,000,000
Service Revenue	$100,000	$200,000	$300,000
Total Inflows	$600,000	$1,200,000	$2,300,000
Cash Outflows			
Rent	$50,000	$60,000	$70,000
Salaries	$200,000	$250,000	$300,000
Marketing	$100,000	$150,000	$200,000
Development	$100,000	$120,000	$140,000
Utilities	$10,000	$12,000	$14,000
Miscellaneous	$5,000	$6,000	$7,000
Total Outflows	$465,000	$598,000	$731,000
Net Cash Flow	$135,000	$602,000	$1,569,000

XYZ Tech Solutions Balance Sheet

Category	Year 1	Year 2	Year 3
Assets			
Cash	$100,000	$300,000	$600,000
Accounts Receivable	$50,000	$100,000	$200,000
Inventory	$20,000	$30,000	$40,000
Equipment	$50,000	$60,000	$70,000
Total Assets	$220,000	$490,000	$910,000
Liabilities			
Accounts Payable	$30,000	$40,000	$50,000
Loans	$50,000	$60,000	$70,000
Total Liabilities	$80,000	$100,000	$120,000
Equity			
Owner's Equity	$140,000	$390,000	$790,000
Total Equity	$140,000	$390,000	$790,000
Total Liabilities and Equity	$220,000	$490,000	$910,000

Developing a comprehensive business plan is crucial for the success of your venture. By including the essential elements outlined in this chapter, you can create a solid foundation for your business and attract potential investors and stakeholders. By following these guidelines and using the provided templates and checklists, you will be well-equipped to develop a business plan that sets your business up for success.

Thank You for your help

If this book gave you value, even in a small way, I need your help.

Amazon reviews are what determine whether this book reaches more people or gets buried. Your voice directly impacts that.

It takes less than 60 seconds.

You don't need to write anything long—just be honest:

- What did you like?
- What stood out?
- Would you recommend it?

That's it.

Leave your review here

Or Scan the QR Code

- Open Your Camera app
- Point Your Mobile device at the QR Code below
- The Review Page appear in your web browser.

I read every single review, and I truly appreciate yours.

Thank you for being part of this journey—and for helping others discover what you just learned.

CHAPTER 6: LEGAL SETUP AND REGISTRATION

Setting up your business legally is a crucial step in establishing a solid foundation for your venture. This chapter will guide you through the essential aspects of legal setup and registration, from choosing the right business structure to ensuring legal compliance. By following the detailed steps and checklists provided, you can navigate the legal landscape with confidence and set your business up for success.

Choosing the Right Business Structure

What Are the Different Types of Business Structures?

Choosing the right business structure is one of the first and most important decisions you'll make when starting your business. The structure you choose will affect your legal responsibilities, taxes, and personal liability.

Sole Proprietorship

- A sole proprietorship is the simplest and most common form of business ownership. It is owned and operated by one individual.
- **Pros**: Easy to set up, complete control of the business, and straightforward tax filing.
- **Cons**: Unlimited personal liability, difficulty in raising capital, and less credibility.

Partnership

- A partnership involves two or more individuals who share ownership of a business. There are two main types of partnerships: general partnerships and limited partnerships.
- **Pros**: Easy to establish, shared financial commitment, and combined expertise and resources.
- **Cons**: Joint liability, potential for conflicts, and profit-sharing.

Limited Liability Company (LLC)

- An LLC is a hybrid structure that combines the benefits of a corporation and a partnership or sole proprietorship. Owners are referred to as members.
- **Pros**: Limited personal liability, flexible management structure, and pass-through taxation.
- **Cons**: It can be more complex and expensive to establish, there are varying state laws, and there is limited life.

Corporation

- A corporation is a separate legal entity owned by shareholders. There are two main types: C corporations and S corporations.
- **Pros**: Limited liability, ability to raise capital through stock, and perpetual existence.
- **Cons**: More complex and costly to set up, double taxation for C corporations, and more regulatory requirements.

S Corporation

- An S corporation is a special type of corporation that allows profits to pass through to the owner's income without being subject to corporate tax rates.

- **Pros**: Limited liability, pass-through taxation, and avoidance of double taxation.
- **Cons**: Restrictions on the number and type of shareholders and more formalities than an LLC.

Nonprofit Organization

- A nonprofit organization is created for charitable, educational, religious, or other public service purposes. It is exempt from paying taxes on income related to its nonprofit purpose.
- **Pros**: Tax-exempt status, eligibility for grants and donations, and limited liability.
- **Cons**: Strict compliance with regulations, complex setup process, and limitations on political and lobbying activities.

How To Choose the Best Structure for Your Business

Selecting the best business structure depends on several factors, including the nature of your business, your goals, and your financial situation. Consider the following when making your decision:

1. **Liability**: Assess your risk tolerance. If you want to protect your assets from business liabilities, consider an LLC or corporation.
2. **Taxes**: Understand the tax implications of each structure. A sole proprietorship or partnership offers pass-through taxation, while a corporation may face double taxation unless it's an S corporation.
3. **Control**: Decide how much control you want over your business. Sole proprietorships and LLCs offer more control, while corporations require a board of directors.
4. **Capital Needs**: Consider how you plan to raise capital. Corporations can issue stock to attract investors, while sole proprietorships and partnerships may have limited funding options.
5. **Complexity and Cost**: Evaluate the complexity and cost of setting up and maintaining each structure. Sole proprietorships are easy and

inexpensive to establish, while corporations are more complex and costly.

6. **Future Goals**: Think about your long-term goals. If you plan to scale your business significantly or go public, a corporation may be the best choice.

Checklist for Selecting a Business Structure

Assess Liability

- Consider the level of personal liability protection you need.
- Evaluate the potential risks associated with your business.

Understand Taxes

- Research the tax implications of each business structure.
- Consult with a tax advisor to understand your specific situation.

Determine Control

- Decide how much control you want over your business.
- Consider the management structure and decision-making processes.

Consider Capital Needs

- Evaluate your funding requirements and potential sources of capital.
- Determine if you need to attract investors or issue stock.

Evaluate Complexity and Cost

- Research the setup and maintenance costs for each structure.
- Consider the administrative and regulatory requirements.

Think About Future Goals

- Consider your long-term business goals and growth plans.
- Choose a structure that aligns with your vision for the future.

Legal Requirements for Business Registration

What Steps Are Involved in Registering a Business?

Registering your business is a crucial step to ensure that it is legally recognized and can operate without legal issues. Here are the general steps involved in registering a business:

Choose a Business Name

- Select a unique and memorable name that reflects your brand and complies with your state's naming rules.
- Check the availability of the name through your state's business registration office or website.

Determine Your Business Structure

- Decide on the best business structure for your venture (e.g., sole proprietorship, LLC, corporation).
- Follow the specific registration requirements for your chosen structure.

Register with State Agencies

- Register your business name and structure with the appropriate state agencies.
- File the necessary documents, such as Articles of Incorporation for a corporation or Articles of Organization for an LLC.

Obtain Business Licenses and Permits

- Determine the licenses and permits required for your business based on your industry and location.
- Apply for and obtain the necessary licenses and permits to operate legally.

Register for Taxes

- Apply for an Employer Identification Number (EIN) from the IRS for tax purposes.
- Register for state and local taxes, including sales tax, if applicable.

Comply with Local Zoning Laws

- Check local zoning regulations to ensure your business location complies with zoning laws.
- Obtain any necessary zoning permits or approvals.

Set Up Business Banking

- Open a dedicated business bank account to separate personal and business finances.
- Choose a bank and account type that meets your business needs.

How Can Entrepreneurs Ensure They Meet All Legal Requirements?

Meeting all legal requirements involves thorough research, careful planning, and attention to detail. Here are some tips to help ensure compliance:

Research Requirements

- Conduct thorough research on federal, state, and local requirements for your industry and location.
- Use reliable sources, such as government websites and legal advisors.

Create a Checklist

- Develop a detailed checklist of all the steps and documents required for registration and compliance.
- Use this checklist to track your progress and ensure nothing is overlooked.

Seek Professional Advice

- Consult with legal and tax professionals to ensure you understand and meet all legal obligations.
- Consider hiring a business attorney to assist with the registration process.

Stay Informed

- Keep up-to-date with changes in laws and regulations that may affect your business.
- Subscribe to industry newsletters and join professional associations for updates.

Step-by-Step Guide for Business Registration

Choose a Business Name

- Research and select a unique business name.
- Check your state's business registration office for name availability.

Determine Your Business Structure

- Decide on the best structure for your business.
- Follow the registration requirements for your chosen structure.

Register with State Agencies

- File Articles of Incorporation (for corporations) or Articles of Organization (for LLCs) with the state.
- Pay the required filing fees.

Obtain Business Licenses and Permits

- Identify the necessary licenses and permits for your business.
- Apply for and obtain the required licenses and permits.

Register for Taxes

- Apply for an EIN from the IRS.
- Register for state and local taxes, including sales tax.

Comply with Local Zoning Laws

- Check zoning regulations for your business location.
- Obtain necessary zoning permits or approvals.

Set Up Business Banking

- Open a business bank account.
- Choose the right bank and account type.

Obtaining an Employer Identification Number (EIN)

Why Is an EIN Important?

An Employer Identification Number (EIN) is a unique identifier assigned by the IRS to businesses for tax purposes. It is essential for several reasons:

1. **Tax Reporting**: An EIN is required for filing federal tax returns, paying taxes, and reporting employee wages.
2. **Business Banking**: Most banks require an EIN to open a business bank

account.

3. **Hiring Employees**: An EIN is necessary for reporting payroll taxes and complying with employment regulations.
4. **Legal Compliance**: An EIN is often required to obtain business licenses and permits.
5. **Credibility**: Having an EIN adds credibility to your business and separates your personal and business finances.

How To Obtain an EIN for Your Business?

Obtaining an EIN is a straightforward process that can be completed online, by mail, fax, or phone. Here's how to apply:

Determine Eligibility

- Ensure your business is eligible for an EIN. Most businesses, including sole proprietorships, partnerships, LLCs, and corporations, qualify.

Gather Required Information

- Business name and address
- Type of business entity
- Reason for applying (e.g., starting a new business, hiring employees)
- Name and Social Security Number (SSN) of the responsible party

Apply Online

- Visit the IRS EIN application page.
- Complete the online application by providing the required information.
- Receive your EIN immediately upon completion.

Apply by Mail or Fax

- Complete Form SS-4, Application for Employer Identification Number.

- Mail or fax the form to the IRS. Mailing addresses and fax numbers are provided in the instructions on the form.
- Receive your EIN by mail within 4-5 weeks (mail) or 4 business days (fax).

Apply by Phone (International Applicants)

- International applicants can apply by phone by calling the IRS at 1-267-941-1099.
- Provide the required information to the IRS representative.
- Receive your EIN immediately.

Step-by-Step Guide for EIN Application

Determine Eligibility

- Verify that your business is eligible for an EIN.

Gather Required Information

- Business name and address
- Type of business entity
- Reason for applying
- Name and SSN of the responsible party

Choose Application Method

- Online: Visit the IRS EIN application page and complete the online application.
- Mail: Complete Form SS-4 and mail it to the IRS.
- Fax: Complete Form SS-4 and fax it to the IRS.
- Phone: Call the IRS at 1-267-941-1099 (for international applicants).

Complete the Application

- Provide the required information accurately.
- Submit the application through your chosen method.

Receive Your EIN

- Online: Receive your EIN immediately.
- Mail: Receive your EIN by mail within 4-5 weeks.
- Fax: Receive your EIN by fax within 4 business days.
- Phone: Receive your EIN immediately.

Setting Up Business Bank Accounts

What Are the Benefits of Having a Dedicated Business Bank Account?

Opening a dedicated business bank account is essential for managing your business finances effectively. Here are the key benefits:

1. **Separation of Finances**: Keeping your personal and business finances separate simplifies accounting and reduces the risk of legal issues.
2. **Professionalism**: A business bank account adds credibility and professionalism to your business, making it easier to build trust with clients and suppliers.
3. **Tax Compliance**: Separate accounts simplify tax reporting and help ensure compliance with tax regulations.
4. **Simplified Accounting**: A dedicated account streamlines bookkeeping and financial management, making it easier to track income and expenses.
5. **Access to Financial Services**: Business bank accounts often come with additional financial services, such as business loans, credit lines, and merchant services.

How To Choose the Right Bank and Account Type?

Choosing the right bank and account type involves evaluating your business needs, comparing options, and considering factors such as fees, services, and convenience. Here's how to choose:

Evaluate Your Needs

- Determine your business's financial needs, including transaction volume, cash flow, and required services.
- Consider whether you need additional services, such as credit lines, loans, or merchant accounts.

Research Banks

- Compare banks based on their reputation, customer service, and available services.
- Consider both local banks and larger national or online banks.

Compare Account Types

- Review the features of different business bank accounts, including checking, savings, and merchant accounts.
- Compare fees, transaction limits, interest rates, and other terms.

Visit Bank Branches

- Visit bank branches to speak with representatives, ask questions, and gather information.
- Evaluate the convenience of the bank's locations and hours.

Read Reviews and Testimonials

- Read reviews and testimonials from other business owners to learn about their experiences with different banks.

Make a Decision

- Choose the bank and account type that best meets your business needs.
- Ensure that the account offers the services and features you require.

Checklist for Setting Up Business Bank Accounts

Evaluate Your Needs

- Determine your business's financial needs.
- Consider additional services required.

Research Banks

- Compare banks based on reputation and services.
- Consider local, national, and online banks.

Compare Account Types

- Review features of different business bank accounts.
- Compare fees, transaction limits, and interest rates.

Visit Bank Branches

- Speak with bank representatives.
- Evaluate convenience and customer service.

Read Reviews and Testimonials

- Read reviews from other business owners.
- Consider their experiences and feedback.

Make a Decision

- Choose the bank and account type that best meets your needs.
- Ensure the account offers the required services and features.

Ensuring Legal Compliance

What Are Common Legal Compliance Issues New Businesses Face?

Legal compliance is critical for avoiding penalties, fines, and legal issues. New businesses often face several common legal compliance challenges, including:

1. **Licensing and Permits**: Failing to obtain the necessary licenses and permits for your industry and location.
2. **Employment Laws**: Violating employment laws, including wage and hour laws, anti-discrimination regulations, and workplace safety standards.
3. **Tax Compliance**: Failing to register for and pay required federal, state, and local taxes, including income tax, sales tax, and payroll taxes.
4. **Intellectual Property**: Infringing on intellectual property rights, such as trademarks, copyrights, and patents.
5. **Zoning Laws**: Operating in a location that does not comply with local zoning regulations.
6. **Privacy and Data Security**: Failing to protect customer data and comply with privacy laws and regulations.

How To Stay Compliant with Regulations?

Staying compliant with regulations involves proactive planning, continuous monitoring, and staying informed about legal requirements. Here are some tips to ensure compliance:

Research Regulations

- Conduct thorough research on federal, state, and local regulations that apply to your business.

- Use reliable sources, such as government websites and legal advisors.

Create a Compliance Plan

- Develop a detailed compliance plan that outlines the steps required to meet legal obligations.
- Assign responsibilities and deadlines to ensure timely compliance.

Stay Informed

- Keep up-to-date with changes in laws and regulations that may affect your business.
- Subscribe to industry newsletters and join professional associations for updates.

Conduct Regular Audits

- Perform regular internal audits to ensure compliance with regulations.
- Identify and address any compliance gaps or issues.

Consult with Professionals

- Seek advice from legal, tax, and compliance professionals to ensure you meet all legal requirements.
- Consider hiring a compliance officer or consultant if needed.

Implement Training Programs

- Provide training for employees on legal compliance and regulatory requirements.
- Ensure that employees understand and follow company policies and procedures.

Checklist for Legal Compliance

Research Regulations

- Identify federal, state, and local regulations that apply to your business.
- Use reliable sources for information.

Create a Compliance Plan

- Develop a detailed compliance plan.
- Assign responsibilities and deadlines.

Stay Informed

- Keep up-to-date with changes in laws and regulations.
- Subscribe to industry newsletters and join professional associations.

Conduct Regular Audits

- Perform regular internal audits.
- Address any compliance gaps or issues.

Consult with Professionals

- Seek advice from legal, tax, and compliance professionals.
- Consider hiring a compliance officer or consultant.

Implement Training Programs

- Provide training for employees on legal compliance.
- Ensure employees understand and follow company policies.

By following the guidelines and checklists provided in this chapter, you can navigate the legal setup and registration process with confidence. Choosing the right business structure, meeting legal requirements, obtaining an EIN, setting up business bank accounts, and ensuring legal compliance are essential steps to establishing a strong foundation for your business. With a solid legal framework in place, you can focus on growing your business and achieving your entrepreneurial goals.

CHAPTER 7: BUILDING AND TESTING YOUR MINIMUM VIABLE PRODUCT (MVP)

Developing a Minimum Viable Product (MVP) is a critical step in the entrepreneurial journey. An MVP allows you to test your business idea, gather valuable feedback, and make necessary adjustments before a full-scale launch. This chapter will guide you through understanding the MVP concept, steps to identify and develop your MVP, learning from successful examples, and iterating based on feedback.

Understanding the MVP Concept

What is a Minimum Viable Product (MVP)?

A Minimum Viable Product (MVP) is the most basic version of a product that allows you to test your business idea with the least amount of effort and resources. It includes only the core features necessary to solve the problem for early adopters and gather feedback for future development. The primary purpose of an MVP is to validate your assumptions and learn what works and what doesn't without investing too much time or money.

Why is it Important to Start with an MVP?

Starting with an MVP is crucial for several reasons:

1. **Risk Reduction**: An MVP helps minimize the risk of failure by allowing you to test your business idea in the real market with minimal invest-

ment.

2. **Market Validation**: It enables you to validate your assumptions about the market demand and customer preferences before committing significant resources.

3. **Learning and Iteration**: By gathering feedback from early adopters, you can learn what features are valuable and necessary, allowing you to iterate and improve your product effectively.

4. **Resource Efficiency**: Developing an MVP ensures that you focus on the most critical features, saving time and resources that might otherwise be spent on unnecessary functionalities.

5. **Early Revenue Generation**: An MVP can help you generate early revenue, which can be reinvested into further development and scaling of your product.

Checklist for Developing an MVP

Identify the Core Problem

- Clearly define the problem your product aims to solve.
- Ensure the problem is significant enough to warrant a solution.

Define the Target Audience

- Identify your ideal customers and their specific needs.
- Conduct market research to validate your target audience.

List Essential Features

- Identify the core features that address the main problem.
- Prioritize features based on their importance and feasibility.

Develop a Prototype

- Create a simple prototype to visualize your MVP.
- Use wireframes, mockups, or a basic version of the product.

Set Success Criteria

- Define the metrics and key performance indicators (KPIs) to measure the success of your MVP.
- Establish clear goals for user engagement, feedback, and validation.

Plan for Feedback Collection

- Develop a strategy to gather feedback from early users.
- Use surveys, interviews, and analytics to collect insights.

Iterate and Improve

- Analyze the feedback and identify areas for improvement.
- Make necessary adjustments and enhancements to the MVP.

Steps to Identify and Develop Your MVP

How To Identify Key Features for Your MVP?

Identifying key features for your MVP involves understanding the core problem you are solving and determining the minimum set of features required to address that problem effectively. Here are the steps to identify key features:

1. **Define the Problem**: Clearly articulate the problem your product aims to solve and why it is important.
2. **Understand Your Audience**: Identify your target customers and understand their pain points, needs, and preferences.
3. **Brainstorm Solutions**: Generate a list of potential features and solutions that address the core problem.

4. **Prioritize Features**: Rank the features based on their importance, feasibility, and impact on solving the problem.
5. **Focus on Core Functionality**: Select the minimum set of features that provide the most value to your target customers.

What Steps Are Involved in Developing and Launching an MVP?

Developing and launching an MVP involves several key steps, from initial planning to collecting feedback post-launch. Here is a step-by-step guide:

Market Research

- Conduct thorough market research to validate the demand for your product.
- Analyze competitors and identify gaps in the market.

Define the MVP Scope

- Clearly define the scope of your MVP, focusing on the core features that address the main problem.
- Set realistic goals and timelines for development.

Create a Prototype

- Develop a basic prototype to visualize the MVP.
- Use wireframes, mockups, or a simple version of the product to gather initial feedback.

Build the MVP

- Develop the MVP with the core features identified.
- Ensure the product is functional, user-friendly, and addresses the main problem effectively.

Test the MVP

- Conduct internal testing to identify and fix any bugs or issues.
- Ensure the MVP meets the defined success criteria and is ready for launch.

Launch the MVP

- Launch the MVP to a select group of early adopters or a small target market.
- Use marketing strategies to attract users and generate interest.

Collect Feedback

- Gather feedback from early users through surveys, interviews, and analytics.
- Analyze the feedback to identify areas for improvement and additional features.

Iterate and Improve

- Make necessary adjustments and enhancements based on user feedback.
- Continue to iterate and improve the product to meet customer needs better.

Step-by-Step Guide for MVP Development

Conduct Market Research

- Validate the demand for your product.
- Analyze competitors and identify market gaps.

Define the MVP Scope

- Focus on core features that solve the main problem.
- Set goals and timelines for development.

Create a Prototype

- Develop a basic prototype using wireframes or mockups.
- Gather initial feedback to refine the design.

Build the MVP

- Develop the MVP with essential features.
- Ensure the product is functional and user-friendly.**Test the MVP**
- Conduct internal testing to identify and fix issues.
- Ensure the MVP meets success criteria.

Launch the MVP

- Launch to a select group of early adopters.
- Use marketing strategies to attract users.

Collect Feedback

- Gather feedback through surveys, interviews, and analytics.
- Analyze feedback to identify improvements.

Iterate and Improve

- Make adjustments based on user feedback.
- Continue to iterate and enhance the product.

Real-Life Examples of Successful MVPs

Dropbox

- **Problem**: Users needed an easy way to store and share files online.
- **Solution**: Dropbox started with a simple MVP—a video demo explaining the product's functionality.
- **Outcome**: The video generated significant interest and validated the demand, leading to further development and a successful launch.

Airbnb

- **Problem**: Travelers needed affordable accommodation options, and homeowners had extra space.
- **Solution**: Airbnb's MVP was a simple website that allowed users to book rooms in their homes.
- **Outcome**: The MVP validated the business model and user demand, leading to rapid growth and expansion.

Zappos

- **Problem**: Customers wanted to buy shoes online but needed clarification about the selection and quality.
- **Solution**: Zappos' MVP involved listing shoes online, purchasing them from local stores, and shipping them to customers.
- **Outcome**: This approach validated the market demand and led to the development of a full-scale e-commerce platform.

What Can Be Learned from Their Experiences?

1. **Start Simple**: Begin with a basic version of your product that solves the core problem.
2. **Validate Demand**: Use the MVP to test market demand and gather

feedback.

3. **Iterate Based on Feedback**: Continuously improve the product based on user insights.

4. **Focus on the Core Problem**: Ensure the MVP addresses the primary issue effectively.

Case Study of a Successful MVP

Case Study: Buffer

- **Problem**: Social media users needed an easy way to schedule posts across multiple platforms.
- **MVP Approach**: Buffer's founder created a simple landing page explaining the product and asking users to sign up if interested.
- **Outcome**: The initial response validated the demand, leading to the development of the first version of Buffer. Today, Buffer is a leading social media management tool with millions of users.

Iteration and Improvement Based on Feedback

How To Gather and Analyze Feedback on Their MVP?

Gathering and analyzing feedback is essential for improving your MVP and ensuring it meets customer needs. Here are some methods to gather feedback:

Surveys and Questionnaires

- Distribute surveys to gather quantitative data on user satisfaction, preferences, and pain points.
- Use tools like Google Forms, SurveyMonkey, or Typeform to create and distribute surveys.

User Interviews

- Conduct one-on-one interviews with users to gather qualitative insights.
- Ask open-ended questions to understand their experiences and suggestions.

Analytics Tools

- Analytics tools like Google Analytics, Mixpanel, or Hotjar can be used to track user behavior and engagement.
- Analyze data on user interactions, feature usage, and drop-off points.

Feedback Forms

- Include feedback forms within your product to collect user comments and suggestions.
- Encourage users to provide feedback after key interactions or at the end of their session.

User Testing

- Conduct user testing sessions to observe how users interact with your product.
- Identify usability issues and areas for improvement.

What Steps Should Be Taken to Iterate and Improve the Product?

Iterating and improving your MVP based on feedback involves several key steps:

Analyze Feedback

- Review and categorize feedback to identify common themes and issues.
- Prioritize feedback based on its impact on user satisfaction and product performance.

Develop an Improvement Plan

- Create a plan to address the most critical feedback and implement necessary changes.
- Set clear goals and timelines for each iteration.

Implement Changes

- Make the necessary updates and improvements to your product.
- Ensure changes are tested thoroughly before releasing them to users.

Communicate with Users

- Inform users about the changes and improvements made based on their feedback.
- Highlight how the updates enhance their experience and address their concerns.

Repeat the Process

- Continue to gather feedback and iterate on your product.
- Use each iteration as an opportunity to refine and enhance your offering.

Checklist for Feedback Analysis and Product Iteration

Gather Feedback

- Distribute surveys and questionnaires.
- Conduct user interviews.
- Use analytics tools to track user behavior.
- Include feedback forms within the product.
- Conduct user testing sessions.

Analyze Feedback

- Review and categorize feedback.
- Identify common themes and issues.
- Prioritize feedback based on impact.

Develop an Improvement Plan

- Create a plan to address critical feedback.
- Set goals and timelines for each iteration.

Implement Changes

- Make necessary updates and improvements.
- Test changes thoroughly before release.

Communicate with Users

- Inform users about changes and improvements.
- Highlight how updates enhance their experience.

Repeat the Process

- Continue gathering feedback.
- Iterate and refine the product based on user insights.

Building and testing your MVP is a crucial step in the entrepreneurial journey. By understanding the MVP concept, identifying key features, learning from successful examples, and iterating based on feedback, you can develop a product that meets customer needs and achieves market success. Use the checklists and step-by-step guides provided in this chapter to navigate the MVP development process and set your business up for long-term success.

CHAPTER 8: BRANDING AND MARKETING STRATEGIES

In today's competitive business landscape, effective branding and marketing strategies are essential for success. This chapter will guide you through establishing a strong brand identity, crafting a unique selling proposition, creating a comprehensive marketing plan, leveraging social media and digital marketing, understanding SEO, comparing advertising platforms, and learning from real-life marketing challenges.

Establishing Your Brand Identity

What Elements Contribute to a Strong Brand Identity?

A strong brand identity is the cornerstone of your business's success. It encompasses everything that makes your brand unique and recognizable. Key elements of a strong brand identity include:

1. **Brand Name**: A unique and memorable name that reflects your brand's values and mission.
2. **Logo**: A visually appealing and easily recognizable logo that represents your brand.
3. **Tagline**: A short, catchy phrase that encapsulates your brand's essence.
4. **Brand Colors**: A consistent color palette that evokes specific emotions and aligns with your brand's personality.
5. **Typography**: The fonts and styles used in your brand's communications

should be consistent and reflective of your brand's tone.

6. **Voice and Tone**: The way your brand communicates with its audience, including the language, style, and personality conveyed.

7. **Brand Story**: The narrative that explains your brand's origins, mission, and values, helping to create an emotional connection with your audience.

How To Develop a Unique and Memorable Brand?

Developing a unique and memorable brand involves a strategic approach that considers your target audience, market position, and brand values. Here are the steps to develop a strong brand identity:

Define Your Brand's Purpose and Values

- Identify your brand's core purpose and the values that guide your business.
- Ensure that these values resonate with your target audience.

Understand Your Target Audience

- Conduct market research to understand your target audience's needs, preferences, and behaviors.
- Create detailed buyer personas to represent your ideal customers.

Analyze Competitors

- Study your competitors to identify their strengths and weaknesses.
- Determine what sets your brand apart and how you can position yourself uniquely in the market.

Create a Unique Brand Name and Logo

- Choose a brand name that is memorable, easy to pronounce, and relevant

114

to your business.
- Design a logo that visually represents your brand and stands out in the market.

Develop a Consistent Brand Voice and Tone

- Define the language, style, and personality your brand will use in all communications.
- Ensure consistency across all platforms and marketing materials.

Craft Your Brand Story

- Develop a compelling narrative that tells the story of your brand's origins, mission, and values.
- Use your brand story to connect with your audience on an emotional level.

Implement Brand Guidelines

- Create a brand style guide that outlines the rules for using your brand elements consistently.
- Ensure that all team members and partners adhere to these guidelines.

Checklist for Brand Identity Development

Define Purpose and Values

- Identify core purpose and values.
- Ensure alignment with the target audience.

Understand Target Audience

- Conduct market research.
- Create detailed buyer personas.

Analyze Competitors

- Study competitors' strengths and weaknesses.
- Determine unique market position.

Create Brand Name and Logo

- Choose a memorable and relevant brand name.
- Design a visually appealing logo.

Develop Brand Voice and Tone

- Define language, style, and personality.
- Ensure consistency across all communications.

Craft Brand Story

- Develop a compelling brand narrative.
- Connect with the audience emotionally.

Implement Brand Guidelines

- Create a brand style guide.
- Ensure adherence to guidelines.

Crafting a Unique Selling Proposition

What is a Unique Selling Proposition (USP)?

A Unique Selling Proposition (USP) is a distinctive feature or benefit that sets your product or service apart from the competition. It answers the question, "Why should customers choose your product over others?" A strong USP highlights the unique value your product offers and resonates with your target audience.

How Can Businesses Create an Effective USP?

Creating an effective USP involves understanding your customers' needs, analyzing your competitors, and clearly articulating what makes your product unique. Here are the steps to develop a compelling USP:

Identify Customer Pain Points

- Understand the challenges and pain points your target audience faces.
- Determine how your product addresses these issues better than competitors.

Analyze Competitors

- Study your competitors to identify their USPs and market positioning.
- Find gaps in the market where your product can offer unique value.

Highlight Unique Features and Benefits

- Identify the key features and benefits of your product that set it apart.
- Focus on what makes your product better, faster, cheaper, or more innovative.

Keep it Clear and Concise.

- Craft a USP that is easy to understand and remember.
- Avoid jargon and complex language; be straightforward and direct.

Test and Refine Your USP

- Test your USP with your target audience to gauge their response.
- Refine your USP based on feedback to ensure it resonates with your customers.

Examples of Strong USPs

1. **FedEx**: "When it absolutely, positively has to be there overnight." – This USP emphasizes reliability and speed, appealing to customers who need urgent deliveries.
2. **Domino's Pizza**: "You get fresh, hot pizza delivered to your door in 30 minutes or less – or it's free." – This USP highlights fast delivery and a satisfaction guarantee.
3. **TOMS Shoes**: "With every pair you purchase, TOMS will give a new pair of shoes to a child in need. One for One®." – This USP focuses on social impact and philanthropy.

Creating a Comprehensive Marketing Plan

What Are the Key Components of a Marketing Plan?

A comprehensive marketing plan outlines your marketing strategy and the steps you will take to reach your target audience and achieve your business goals. Key components of a marketing plan include:

1. **Executive Summary**: A brief overview of the marketing plan, including key objectives and strategies.
2. **Market Research**: Analysis of the market, target audience, and competitive landscape.
3. **Marketing Objectives**: Specific, measurable goals that align with your business objectives.
4. **Target Audience**: Detailed descriptions of your ideal customers, including demographics, psychographics, and behaviors.
5. **Positioning Statement**: A clear statement that defines how you want your brand to be perceived in the market.
6. **Marketing Strategies**: The tactics and channels you will use to reach your target audience (e.g., content marketing, social media, email marketing).
7. **Budget**: An outline of the financial resources allocated to marketing

activities.

8. **Metrics and KPIs**: The key performance indicators (KPIs) and metrics you will use to measure the success of your marketing efforts.

How To Develop a Strategy That Reaches Your Target Audience?

Developing an effective marketing strategy involves understanding your audience, setting clear objectives, and choosing the right channels and tactics. Here are the steps to create a marketing strategy:

Conduct Market Research

- Gather data on your target audience, including demographics, preferences, and behaviors.
- Analyze market trends and competitors.

Define Marketing Objectives

- Set specific, measurable, achievable, relevant, and time-bound (SMART) goals.
- Align marketing objectives with your overall business goals.

Identify Your Target Audience

- Create detailed buyer personas that represent your ideal customers.
- Understand their needs, preferences, and pain points.

Develop Positioning Statement

- Define how you want your brand to be perceived in the market.
- Craft a positioning statement that communicates your unique value proposition.

Choose Marketing Channels and Tactics

- Select the channels and tactics that best reach your target audience (e.g., social media, email marketing, content marketing).
- Develop a content calendar and campaign plan.

Allocate Budget

- Determine the financial resources needed for your marketing activities.
- Allocate the budget to different channels and tactics based on their potential ROI.

Measure and Analyze Results

- Use metrics and KPIs to track the performance of your marketing efforts.
- Analyze results and adjust your strategy as needed.

Sample Marketing Plan Template
Executive Summary

- A brief overview of marketing objectives and strategies.

Market Research

- Analysis of target audience and competitors.

Marketing Objectives

- Specific, measurable goals.

Target Audience

- Detailed buyer personas.

Positioning Statement

- A clear statement of brand positioning.

Marketing Strategies

- Tactics and channels to reach the target audience.

Budget

- Financial resources allocated to marketing activities.

Metrics and KPIs

- Key performance indicators to measure success.

Leveraging Social Media and Digital Marketing

How Can Social Media Be Used to Promote a Business?

Social media is a powerful tool for promoting a business, building brand awareness, and engaging with customers. Here are some ways to leverage social media for business promotion:

Create Engaging Content

- Share high-quality, relevant content that resonates with your audience.
- Use a mix of content types, such as images, videos, infographics, and blog posts.

Build a Community

- Foster a sense of community by engaging with your followers and encouraging discussions.
- Respond to comments, messages, and reviews promptly.

Run Contests and Giveaways

- Organize contests and giveaways to increase engagement and attract new followers.
- Encourage participants to share your content and tag their friends.

Use Hashtags

- Use relevant hashtags to increase the visibility of your posts.
- Create branded hashtags to encourage user-generated content.

Collaborate with Influencers

- Partner with influencers in your industry to reach a wider audience.
- Choose influencers whose values align with your brand.

Analyze Performance

- Use social media analytics tools to track the performance of your posts and campaigns.
- Adjust your strategy based on the insights gained.

What Digital Marketing Tactics Are Most Effective?

Effective digital marketing tactics help you reach your target audience, generate leads, and drive conversions. Here are some key tactics to consider:

Content Marketing

- Create valuable content that educates, entertains, or informs your audience.
- Use blog posts, videos, e-books, and webinars to engage and attract customers.

Email Marketing

- Build an email list and send targeted campaigns to nurture leads and retain customers.
- Personalize emails and use automation to improve engagement.

Search Engine Optimization (SEO)

- Optimize your website and content for search engines to improve organic visibility.
- Use keywords, meta tags, and quality backlinks.

Pay-Per-Click (PPC) Advertising

- Use PPC ads to drive targeted traffic to your website.
- Focus on platforms like Google Ads and social media ads.

Social Media Marketing

- Leverage social media platforms to connect with your audience and promote your brand.
- Use a mix of organic posts and paid ads.

Affiliate Marketing

- Partner with affiliates who promote your products in exchange for a commission.
- Track affiliate performance and optimize your program.

Checklist for Social Media and Digital Marketing

Create Engaging Content

- Share high-quality, relevant content.
- Use a mix of content types.

Build a Community

- Engage with followers and encourage discussions.
- Respond to comments and messages.

Run Contests and Giveaways

- Organize contests to increase engagement.
- Encourage sharing and tagging.

Use Hashtags

- Use relevant hashtags to increase visibility.
- Create branded hashtags.

Collaborate with Influencers

- Partner with influencers to reach a wider audience.
- Choose influencers aligned with your brand.

Analyze Performance

- Use analytics tools to track performance.
- Adjust strategy based on insights.

Basics of SEO for Online Presence

What is SEO, and Why is It Important?

Search Engine Optimization (SEO) is the practice of optimizing your website and content to rank higher in search engine results pages (SERPs). SEO is important because:

1. **Increases Visibility**: Higher rankings in search results lead to increased visibility and more organic traffic.
2. **Builds Credibility**: Websites that rank higher are perceived as more credible and trustworthy.
3. **Drives Targeted Traffic**: SEO helps attract users who are actively searching for products or services like yours.
4. **Improves User Experience**: Optimizing your website for SEO often improves the overall user experience.

Basic SEO Strategies to Improve Online Visibility

Keyword Research

- Identify relevant keywords that your target audience is searching for.
- Use tools like Google Keyword Planner, SEMrush, and Ahrefs.

On-Page Optimization

- Optimize title tags, meta descriptions, and headers with targeted keywords.
- Use keywords naturally within your content.

Quality Content Creation

- Create high-quality, valuable content that addresses your audience's needs.
- Use a mix of text, images, and videos.

Technical SEO

- Ensure your website is mobile-friendly and has a fast loading speed.

- Use proper URL structures and sitemaps.

Backlink Building

- Acquire quality backlinks from reputable websites in your industry.
- Use guest blogging, partnerships, and outreach strategies.

Local SEO

- Optimize your Google My Business profile for local search.
- Use local keywords and build citations.

Checklist for SEO Best Practices

Keyword Research

- Identify relevant keywords.
- Use keyword research tools.

On-Page Optimization

- Optimize title tags and meta descriptions.
- Use keywords naturally in content.

Quality Content Creation

- Create valuable, high-quality content.
- Use a mix of text, images, and videos.

Technical SEO

- Ensure mobile-friendliness and fast loading speed.
- Use proper URL structures and sitemaps.

Backlink Building

- Acquire quality backlinks.
- Use guest blogging and outreach.

Local SEO

- Optimize Google My Business profile.
- Use local keywords and build citations.

Comparing Facebook Ads and Google Ads

What Are the Pros and Cons of Facebook Ads vs. Google Ads?

Both Facebook Ads and Google Ads are powerful advertising platforms, but they have different strengths and weaknesses.

Facebook Ads

- **Pros**:
- **Targeting**: Advanced targeting options based on demographics, interests, and behaviors.
- **Engagement**: High engagement rates with visual and interactive ads.
- **Cost-Effective**: Generally lower cost-per-click (CPC) than Google Ads.
- **Cons**:
- **Intent**: Users need to search for products actively; ads may be less relevant.
- **Ad Fatigue**: A high frequency of ads can lead to ad fatigue among users.

Google Ads

- **Pros**:
- **Intent**: Ads appear when users are actively searching for related products or services.
- **Reach:** Large reach through Google's search network and display net-

work.

- **Performance**: Higher conversion rates due to user intent.
- **Cons**:
- **Cost**: Higher CPC, especially for competitive keywords.
- **Complexity**: Requires more expertise to manage and optimize campaigns.

How To Decide Which Platform to Use?

Choosing between Facebook Ads and Google Ads depends on your business goals, target audience, and budget. Here are some factors to consider:

Business Goals

- Use Google Ads if your goal is to capture high-intent traffic and drive conversions.
- Use Facebook Ads for brand awareness, engagement, and reaching a specific audience based on interests and behaviors.

Target Audience

- Choose Facebook Ads if your audience is active on social media and you want to target them based on demographics and interests.
- Choose Google Ads if your audience is actively searching for products or services related to your business.

Budget

- Consider your budget and the cost-per-click for your industry. Facebook Ads can be more cost-effective for smaller budgets.
- Google Ads may require a higher budget, especially for competitive keywords.

Comparison Guide for Facebook Ads and Google Ads

Feature	Facebook Ads	Google Ads
Targeting	Advanced targeting options	Keyword-based targeting
Engagement	High engagement rates	Higher conversion rates
Cost	Lower CPC	Higher CPC
Intent	Lower user intent	Higher user intent
Reach	Large social media audience	Large search and display network
Ad Formats	Visual and interactive ads	Text and display ads
Complexity	Easier to set up and manage	Requires more expertise

Case Study: Marketing Strategy Challenges and Solutions

Case Study: XYZ Fitness

Background: XYZ Fitness is a startup offering online fitness classes and personalized training programs. Despite having a unique offering, they needed help to attract and retain customers.

Challenges:

1. **Low Brand Awareness**: XYZ Fitness was relatively unknown in the crowded fitness market.
2. **Ineffective Marketing Strategy**: Their marketing efforts were scattered and lacked focus.
3. **Poor Engagement**: Social media posts and advertisements were not generating the desired engagement.

Solutions and Outcomes

Solution 1: Rebranding and Identity Development

- **Action**: XYZ Fitness revamped its brand identity with a new logo, tagline, and brand colors that reflected its energetic and modern approach.
- **Outcome**: Improved brand recognition and a more cohesive brand image.

Solution 2: Develop a Unique Selling Proposition (USP)

- **Action**: They identified their USP as "Personalized Fitness Programs Tailored to Your Unique Needs" and highlighted this in all marketing materials.
- **Outcome**: Clear differentiation from competitors and a stronger value proposition.

Solution 3: Creating a Comprehensive Marketing Plan

- **Action**: XYZ Fitness developed a detailed marketing plan that included content marketing, social media, email campaigns, and influencer partnerships.
- **Outcome**: More focused and effective marketing efforts that increased brand awareness and engagement.

Solution 4: Leveraging Social Media and Digital Marketing

- **Action**: They implemented a social media strategy with regular posts, interactive content, and live sessions. They also invested in targeted Facebook and Google Ads.
- **Outcome**: Increased social media engagement, website traffic, and lead generation.

Actionable Insights and Lessons Learned

1. **Brand Consistency**: A strong and consistent brand identity is crucial for recognition and trust.
2. **Clear USP**: Clearly communicating your unique value proposition helps

differentiate your brand.

3. **Strategic Planning**: A well-defined marketing plan ensures focused and effective efforts.

4. **Engagement**: Interactive and engaging content on social media can

CHAPTER 9: SALES AND CUSTOMER RELATIONSHIP MANAGEMENT

In this chapter, we will discuss the essential aspects of building a robust sales strategy, delivering excellent customer service, handling customer feedback to improve products, and creating loyal customers and advocates. By focusing on these key areas, you can enhance your business's growth and ensure long-term success.

Building a Robust Sales Strategy

What Are Key Components of a Successful Sales Strategy?

A successful sales strategy involves a comprehensive plan to identify and convert potential customers into paying clients. Key components of a successful sales strategy include:

1. **Target Market Identification**: Clearly define your target market based on demographics, psychographics, and behavior.
2. **Value Proposition**: Articulate the unique benefits and value your product or service offers to the target market.
3. **Sales Goals**: Set specific, measurable, achievable, relevant, and time-bound (SMART) sales goals.
4. **Sales Channels**: Determine the most effective sales channels (e.g., online, direct sales, retail).
5. **Sales Process**: Develop a step-by-step sales process that includes lead

generation, qualification, nurturing, conversion, and follow-up.

6. **Sales Tools and Technology**: Utilize sales tools and technologies (e.g., CRM systems, sales automation tools) to streamline the sales process.

7. **Performance Metrics**: Establish key performance indicators (KPIs) to measure the effectiveness of your sales strategy.

How To Build and Manage Your Sales Pipeline.

Building and managing a sales pipeline involves creating a systematic approach to track and manage potential customers through different stages of the sales process. Here are the steps to build and manage a sales pipeline:

Lead Generation

- Identify potential customers through various channels such as online marketing, networking events, referrals, and advertising.
- Use lead magnets (e.g., free trials, e-books) to attract and capture leads.

Lead Qualification

- Evaluate leads to determine their potential to become paying customers.
- Use criteria such as budget, authority, need, and timeline (BANT) to qualify leads.

Lead Nurturing

- Develop relationships with leads through personalized communication and content.
- Use email marketing, social media, and follow-up calls to keep leads engaged.

Sales Conversion

- Move-qualified leads through the sales funnel by addressing their needs and objections.

- Use sales techniques such as demonstrations, testimonials, and case studies to persuade leads.

Post-Sales Follow-Up

- Follow up with customers after the sale to ensure satisfaction and address any issues.
- Use follow-up calls, emails, and surveys to gather feedback and build long-term relationships.

Checklist for Sales Strategy Development

Identify Target Market

- Define demographics, psychographics, and behavior.
- Conduct market research to validate your target market.

Articulate Value Proposition

- Clearly communicate the unique benefits and value of your product.
- Ensure it addresses the needs and pain points of your target market.

Set Sales Goals

- Establish SMART sales goals.
- Align goals with overall business objectives.

Determine Sales Channels

- Identify the most effective sales channels for your business.
- Consider online, direct sales, and retail options.

Develop Sales Process

- Create a step-by-step sales process.
- Include lead generation, qualification, nurturing, conversion, and follow-up.

Utilize Sales Tools

- Implement CRM systems and sales automation tools.
- Train your sales team to use these tools effectively.

Establish Performance Metrics

- Define KPIs to measure sales effectiveness.
- Monitor and analyze sales data regularly.

Techniques for Excellent Customer Service

What Are the Best Practices for Delivering Outstanding Customer Service?
Delivering outstanding customer service is crucial for building customer loyalty and driving business growth. Best practices for excellent customer service include:

1. **Active Listening**: Pay close attention to customers' needs, concerns, and feedback.
2. **Empathy**: Show genuine empathy and understanding towards customers' issues and emotions.
3. **Prompt Response**: Respond to customer inquiries and complaints promptly.
4. **Clear Communication**: Communicate clearly and effectively, avoiding jargon and confusion.
5. **Personalization**: Personalize interactions to make customers feel valued and appreciated.

6. **Problem Resolution**: Resolve customer issues quickly and efficiently, going above and beyond to ensure satisfaction.
7. **Follow-Up**: Follow up with customers to ensure their issues have been resolved and they are satisfied with the service.

How Can Businesses Handle Customer Complaints Effectively?

Handling customer complaints effectively involves a structured approach to addressing and resolving issues while maintaining a positive relationship with the customer. Here are the steps to handle customer complaints:

Acknowledge the Complaint

- Listen to the customer's complaint without interrupting.
- Acknowledge their concerns and thank them for bringing the issue to your attention.

Show Empathy

- Express understanding and empathy for the customer's frustration or inconvenience.
- Use phrases like "I understand how you feel" or "I'm sorry for any inconvenience this has caused."

Gather Information

- Ask questions to gather all necessary information about the issue.
- Take notes and ensure you understand the problem fully.

Apologize and Take Responsibility

- Apologize for the issue, even if it was not your fault.
- Take responsibility for resolving the problem.

Offer a Solution

- Propose a solution that addresses the customer's concerns.
- Ensure the solution is practical and feasible.

Implement the Solution

- Take immediate action to resolve the issue.
- Keep the customer informed of the progress.

Follow Up

- Follow up with the customer to ensure they are satisfied with the resolution.
- Ask for feedback on how the situation was handled.

Guide for Customer Service Techniques

Active Listening

- Focus on the customer without distractions.
- Repeat back what the customer says to ensure understanding.

Empathy

- Express genuine concern and understanding.
- Use empathetic language.

Prompt Response

- Respond to inquiries and complaints within 24 hours.
- Use automated responses to acknowledge receipt of the complaint.

Clear Communication

- Use simple and clear language.
- Avoid technical jargon.

Personalization

- Address customers by their name.
- Customize interactions based on customer history and preferences.

Problem Resolution

- Identify the root cause of the issue.
- Offer multiple solutions if possible.

Follow-Up

- Send a follow-up email or call to check on customer satisfaction.
- Ask for feedback on the service experience.

Handling Customer Feedback and Improving Products

Why Is Customer Feedback Important?

Customer feedback is invaluable for understanding how your products or services are perceived and identifying areas for improvement. It provides insights into customer satisfaction, preferences, and pain points, helping you make informed decisions to enhance your offerings.

1. **Improves Products and Services**: Feedback helps identify strengths and weaknesses in your products or services, guiding improvements.
2. **Enhances Customer Experience**: Understanding customer needs and addressing their concerns leads to a better customer experience.
3. **Builds Trust and Loyalty**: Actively seeking and acting on feedback shows

customers that you value their opinions, building trust and loyalty.

4. **Drives Innovation**: Customer suggestions can inspire new ideas and innovations, helping you stay competitive.

How Can Feedback Be Used to Improve Products and Services?

Using feedback to improve products and services involves a systematic approach to collecting, analyzing, and implementing customer insights. Here are the steps to effectively use feedback:

Collect Feedback

- Use multiple channels such as surveys, interviews, social media, and feedback forms.
- Encourage customers to provide honest feedback.

Analyze Feedback

- Categorize feedback into common themes and issues.
- Prioritize feedback based on its impact on customer satisfaction and business goals.

Develop an Action Plan

- Create a plan to address the most critical feedback.
- Set clear goals and timelines for implementing changes.

Implement Changes

- Make necessary improvements to products or services based on the feedback.
- Ensure changes are tested thoroughly before release.

Communicate with Customers

- Inform customers about the changes made based on their feedback.
- Highlight how their input has influenced the improvements.

Monitor Results

- Track the impact of the changes on customer satisfaction and business performance.
- Continue to gather feedback to ensure ongoing improvement.

Checklist for Managing Customer Feedback

Collect Feedback

- Use surveys, interviews, social media, and feedback forms.
- Encourage honest feedback from customers.

Analyze Feedback

- Categorize feedback into common themes.
- Prioritize based on impact.

Develop Action Plan

- Create a plan to address critical feedback.
- Set goals and timelines.

Implement Changes

- Make improvements based on feedback.
- Test changes before release.

Communicate with Customers

- Inform customers about changes made.
- Highlight their influence on improvements.

Monitor Results

- Track the impact of changes.
- Continue to gather feedback.

Creating Loyal Customers and Advocates

What Strategies Can Help Turn Customers into Loyal Advocates?

Turning customers into loyal advocates involves creating a positive customer experience, consistently delivering value, and building strong relationships. Here are some strategies to achieve this:

Deliver Exceptional Customer Service

- Provide outstanding customer service to exceed customer expectations.
- Address issues promptly and efficiently.

Personalize Customer Interactions

- Use customer data to personalize interactions and offers.
- Make customers feel valued and appreciated.

Reward Loyalty

- Implement a customer loyalty program that rewards repeat business.
- Offer exclusive discounts, early access to new products, and special promotions.

Encourage Customer Feedback

- Actively seek feedback and show that you value customers' opinions.
- Use feedback to make continuous improvements.

Build a Community

- Create a community around your brand where customers can interact and share their experiences.
- Use social media, forums, and events to foster community engagement.

Communicate Regularly

- Keep customers informed with regular updates, newsletters, and personalized messages.
- Share relevant and valuable content.

Show Appreciation

- Thank customers for their business and loyalty.
- Send personalized thank-you notes, gifts, or special offers.

How Can Businesses Build Strong Relationships with Their Customers?

Building strong relationships with customers involves ongoing engagement, trust-building, and delivering consistent value. Here are some actionable tips:

Be Transparent

- Communicate openly and honestly with customers.
- Be transparent about your products, services, and policies.

Listen Actively

- Listen to customers' needs, concerns, and feedback.
- Show empathy and understanding.

Provide Consistent Value

- Continuously deliver high-quality products and services.
- Ensure consistency in your offerings.

Engage with Customers

- Interact with customers on social media, by email, and in person.
- Create opportunities for meaningful engagement.

Resolve Issues Quickly

- Address customer complaints and issues promptly.
- Take responsibility and provide effective solutions.

Foster Trust

- Keep promises and meet customer expectations.
- Build trust through reliability and integrity.

Offer Exclusive Benefits

- Provide exclusive benefits to loyal customers.
- Create a sense of exclusivity and reward loyalty.

Actionable Tips for Customer Loyalty Programs

Design a Simple Program

- Create a loyalty program that is easy to understand and use.

- Offer clear and achievable rewards.

Offer Valuable Rewards

- Provide rewards that are valuable and relevant to your customers.
- Include discounts, freebies, and exclusive access.

Promote the Program

- Use marketing channels to promote your loyalty program.
- Highlight the benefits and encourage sign-ups.

Track Participation

- Monitor participation and engagement in your loyalty program.
- Use data to optimize the program and increase its effectiveness.

Engage Regularly

- Communicate regularly with loyalty program members.
- Keep them informed about new rewards and opportunities.

Gather Feedback

- Ask for feedback on the loyalty program.
- Use feedback to make improvements.

Show Appreciation

- Thank loyalty program members for their participation.
- Offer special recognition to top participants.

By focusing on building a robust sales strategy, delivering excellent customer service, effectively handling customer feedback, and creating loyal customers and advocates, you can enhance your business's growth and ensure long-term success. Use the checklists and actionable tips provided in this chapter to implement these strategies and build strong, lasting relationships with your customers.

service, effectively leading customer feedback, and creating loyalty programs and advocates, you can enhance your business's growth and success. long-term success. Use the checklists and actionable tips provided in this chapter to implement these strategies and build a strong, loyal customer base. In

CHAPTER 10: ACCOUNTING AND FINANCIAL MANAGEMENT

Effective accounting and financial management are essential for the sustainability and growth of any business. This chapter will guide you through setting up an accounting system, selecting the right accounting software, managing cash flow and expenses, and understanding financial reports. By mastering these areas, you can ensure your business's financial health and make informed decisions that drive success.

Setting Up an Accounting System

What Are the First Steps in Setting Up an Accounting System?

Setting up an accounting system is the foundation of good financial management. Here are the first steps to establish an effective accounting system:

Understand Your Business Needs

- Assess the size and complexity of your business.
- Identify the specific accounting tasks and reports you need (e.g., invoicing, payroll, financial statements).

Choose Between Cash and Accrual Accounting

- Decide whether to use cash accounting (recording transactions when cash changes hands) or accrual accounting (recording transactions when they occur, regardless of cash flow).
- Accrual accounting is generally recommended for businesses that extend credit to customers or have inventory.

Open a Business Bank Account

- Separate your personal and business finances by opening a dedicated business bank account.
- This helps in accurately tracking and reporting business transactions.

Select Accounting Software

- Choose accounting software that meets your business needs and budget.
- Ensure it has features like invoicing, expense tracking, payroll, and financial reporting.

Set Up a Chart of Accounts

- Create a chart of accounts that categorizes all your business transactions.
- Common categories include assets, liabilities, equity, income, and expenses.

Implement a Record-Keeping System

- Develop a system for organizing and storing financial documents (e.g., receipts, invoices, bank statements).
- Consider both digital and physical storage options.

Hire or Train Accounting Staff

- Depending on your business size, hire a bookkeeper or accountant.

- Alternatively, train yourself or existing staff on basic accounting principles and software usage.

Establish Internal Controls

- Implement internal controls to prevent fraud and ensure accuracy.
- Examples include separation of duties, regular audits, and approval processes for expenses.

Checklist for Setting Up an Accounting System
Understand Business Needs

- Assess business size and complexity.
- Identify required accounting tasks and reports.

Choose Accounting Method

- Decide between cash and accrual accounting.

Open Business Bank Account

- Separate personal and business finances.

Select Accounting Software

- Choose software with essential features.
- Ensure it fits your budget.

Set Up Chart of Accounts

- Categorize transactions into assets, liabilities, equity, income, and expenses.

Implement Record-Keeping System

- Organize and store financial documents.
- Consider digital and physical storage.

Hire or Train Staff

- Hire a bookkeeper or accountant.
- Train staff on accounting principles and software.

Establish Internal Controls

- Implement controls to prevent fraud.
- Conduct regular audits and approval processes.

Selecting the Right Accounting Software

Compare Popular Accounting Software Options

Choosing the right accounting software is critical for efficient financial management. Here are comparisons of some popular accounting software options:

QuickBooks Online

- **Pros**: User-friendly interface, comprehensive features (invoicing, expense tracking, payroll), cloud-based access, integration with third-party apps.
- **Cons**: Higher cost for advanced plans and limited customization.
- **Best For**: Small to medium-sized businesses looking for a robust, all-in-one accounting solution.

Xero

- **Pros**: Intuitive design, strong invoicing and expense management, multi-currency support, excellent customer support.
- **Cons**: Limited payroll functionality in some regions, fewer third-party integrations compared to QuickBooks.
- **Best For**: Small businesses and startups that need simple, effective accounting software.

FreshBooks

- **Pros**: Easy to use, strong invoicing capabilities, time tracking and project management features, mobile app.
- **Cons**: Limited accounting features compared to QuickBooks and Xero, higher cost for advanced plans.
- **Best For**: Freelancers and small businesses that focus on invoicing and project management.

Wave

- **Pros**: Free accounting software, including invoicing and receipt scanning, user-friendly interface.
- **Cons**: Limited features compared to paid software, no dedicated customer support.
- **Best For**: Very small businesses and freelancers looking for a free, basic accounting solution.

Zoho Books

- **Pros**: Affordable pricing, comprehensive features, strong automation capabilities, integration with Zoho suite of apps.
- **Cons**: Steeper learning curve, limited third-party integrations.
- **Best For**: Small businesses that use other Zoho apps and need a cost-effective accounting solution.

How Can Businesses Select the Best One for Their Needs?

Selecting the best accounting software for your business involves evaluating your specific needs, budget, and the features each software offers. Here are the steps to choose the right accounting software:

Identify Business Needs

- Determine the specific accounting tasks and features your business requires (e.g., invoicing, payroll, inventory management).
- Consider the size of your business and the complexity of your transactions.

Evaluate Budget

- Assess your budget for accounting software.
- Compare the costs of different software options and their pricing plans.

Research Software Options

- Research popular accounting software options and their features.
- Read reviews and testimonials from other businesses.

Request Demos and Trials

- Request demos or free trials from shortlisted software providers.
- Test the software to ensure it meets your needs and is user-friendly.

Consider Integration

- Ensure the accounting software integrates with other tools and systems you use (e.g., CRM, e-commerce platforms).
- Check for compatibility with your existing technology stack.

Assess Customer Support

- Evaluate the level of customer support offered by the software provider.
- Consider the availability of support channels (e.g., phone, email, chat) and response times.

Make a Decision

- Choose the accounting software that best fits your needs, budget, and business requirements.
- Ensure it offers scalability to grow with your business.

Comparison Guide for Accounting Software

Feature	QuickBooks Online	Xero	FreshBooks	Wave	Zoho Books
User Interface	User-friendly	Intuitive	Easy to use	User-friendly	Moderate
Invoicing	Comprehensive	Strong	Strong	Basic	Comprehensive
Expense Tracking	Comprehensive	Strong	Limited	Basic	Comprehensive
Payroll	Advanced	Limited in some regions	Limited	None	Comprehensive
Multi-Currency Support	Yes	Yes	No	No	Yes
Integration	Extensive third-party integrations	Moderate	Limited	Basic	Strong within Zoho suite
Customer Support	Moderate	Excellent	Moderate	Limited	Moderate
Price	Higher cost for advanced plans	Moderate	Higher cost for advanced plans	Free	Affordable
Best For	Small to medium-sized businesses	Small businesses and startups	Freelancers and small businesses	Very small businesses and freelancers	Small businesses using Zoho app

Managing Cash Flow and Expenses

Why Is Cash Flow Management Crucial?

Cash flow management is crucial for the financial health and stability of a business. It involves monitoring and optimizing the inflows and outflows of cash to ensure that the business has sufficient funds to meet its obligations and invest in growth opportunities. Key reasons why cash flow management is important include:

1. **Ensures Liquidity**: Proper cash flow management ensures that the business has enough cash to cover day-to-day operations, such as paying employees, suppliers, and bills.
2. **Prevents Insolvency**: Managing cash flow helps avoid situations where the business cannot meet its financial obligations, reducing the risk of insolvency or bankruptcy.
3. **Supports Decision-Making**: Understanding cash flow patterns helps business owners make informed decisions about investments, expenses, and financing.
4. **Facilitates Growth**: Effective cash flow management enables businesses to allocate funds to growth opportunities, such as expanding operations, launching new products, or entering new markets.
5. **Builds Financial Stability**: Maintaining a positive cash flow helps build a strong financial foundation, making it easier to secure loans and attract investors.

Tips for Managing Business Expenses Effectively

Managing business expenses effectively involves controlling costs, optimizing spending, and ensuring that expenditures align with business goals. Here are some tips for managing expenses:

Track Expenses Regularly

- Monitor and record all business expenses accurately.

- Use accounting software to automate expense tracking and generate reports.

Create a Budget

- Develop a detailed budget that outlines expected income and expenses.
- Allocate funds to different categories and stick to the budget.

Reduce Unnecessary Costs

- Identify and eliminate non-essential expenses.
- Negotiate better terms with suppliers and service providers.

Implement Cost Control Measures

- Set spending limits for different departments and activities.
- Use purchase orders and approval processes to control spending.

Optimize Resource Utilization

- Ensure efficient use of resources, such as inventory, equipment, and utilities.
- Implement energy-saving measures and reduce waste.

Monitor Cash Flow

- Regularly review cash flow statements to identify trends and potential issues.
- Adjust spending based on cash flow projections.

Plan for Seasonal Variations

- Anticipate seasonal fluctuations in revenue and expenses.

- Build a cash reserve to cover periods of low cash flow.

Sample Cash Flow Management Plan
1. Cash Flow Forecasting

- Project future cash inflows and outflows based on historical data and business plans.
- Use accounting software to create cash flow forecasts.

2. Managing Receivables

- Implement clear payment terms and policies for customers.
- Follow up on overdue invoices promptly.

3. Controlling Payables

- Negotiate favorable payment terms with suppliers.
- Schedule payments to optimize cash flow.

4. Maintaining a Cash Reserve

- Set aside a portion of profits as a cash reserve.
- Use the reserve to cover unexpected expenses or cash flow shortfalls.

5. Regular Monitoring and Review

- Review cash flow statements regularly to identify trends and issues.
- Adjust cash flow management strategies as needed.

6. Investing Surplus Cash

- Identify opportunities to invest surplus cash for higher returns.
- Ensure investments are liquid and align with business goals.

Understanding Financial Reports

What Are the Key Financial Reports Every Business Should Understand?

Understanding key financial reports is essential for making informed business decisions. The main financial reports every business should understand include:

Income Statement (Profit and Loss Statement)

- **Purpose**: Shows the business's revenues, expenses, and profits over a specific period.
- **Key Components**: Revenues, cost of goods sold (COGS), gross profit, operating expenses, net income.

Balance Sheet

- **Purpose**: Provides a snapshot of the business's financial position at a specific point in time.
- **Key Components**: Assets, liabilities, equity.

Cash Flow Statement

- **Purpose**: Shows the cash inflows and outflows from operating, investing, and financing activities over a specific period.
- **Key Components**: Operating cash flow, investing cash flow, financing cash flow, net change in cash.

Statement of Retained Earnings

- **Purpose**: Shows the changes in retained earnings over a specific period.
- **Key Components**: Beginning retained earnings, net income, dividends, ending retained earnings.

How To Use These Reports to Make Informed Decisions?

Using financial reports effectively involves analyzing the data to understand the business's performance and making decisions that drive growth and profitability. Here's how to use each report:

Income Statement Analysis

- **Revenue Trends**: Analyze revenue trends to identify growth patterns and areas for improvement.
- **Expense Management**: Review expenses to identify cost-saving opportunities and optimize spending.
- **Profitability**: Assess profitability by comparing net income with industry benchmarks and historical performance.

Balance Sheet Analysis

- **Liquidity**: Evaluate liquidity by analyzing current assets and liabilities to ensure the business can meet short-term obligations.
- **Leverage**: Assess the level of debt and equity to understand the business's financial stability and risk.
- **Asset Management**: Review asset utilization to ensure efficient use of resources and investments.

Cash Flow Statement Analysis

- **Operating Cash Flow**: Monitor cash flow from operations to ensure the business generates sufficient cash to cover expenses.
- **Investment Decisions**: Use investing cash flow to evaluate capital expenditures and investment strategies.
- **Financing Activities**: Analyze financing cash flow to understand how the business is funded and managed.

Statement of Retained Earnings Analysis

- **Profit Reinvestment**: Review retained earnings to understand how profits are reinvested in the business.
- **Dividend Policy**: Assess the impact of dividend payments on retained earnings and growth.

Guide for Interpreting Financial Reports

Income Statement

- **Revenue Analysis**: Compare current revenues with previous periods and industry benchmarks.
- **Expense Analysis**: Identify major expense categories and analyze trends.
- **Profitability**: Calculate key ratios such as gross profit margin, operating profit margin, and net profit margin.

Balance Sheet

- **Current Ratio**: Calculate the current ratio (current assets/current liabilities) to assess liquidity.
- **Debt-to-Equity Ratio**: Calculate the debt-to-equity ratio (total liabilities/total equity) to evaluate leverage.
- **Asset Turnover**: Calculate the asset turnover ratio (revenue/total assets) to assess asset efficiency.

Cash Flow Statement

- **Operating Cash Flow**: Compare operating cash flow with net income to assess cash generation.
- **Capital Expenditures**: Analyze investing cash flow for capital expenditures and long-term investments.
- **Debt Management**: Review financing cash flow for debt repayments and financing activities.

Statement of Retained Earnings

- **Profit Reinvestment**: Analyze the proportion of profits reinvested in the business.
- **Dividend Policy**: Assess the impact of dividends on retained earnings and growth.

By setting up an effective accounting system, selecting the right accounting software, managing cash flow and expenses, and understanding key financial reports, you can ensure your business's financial health and make informed decisions that drive success. Use the checklists and guides provided in this chapter to implement best practices in accounting and financial management.

CHAPTER 11: GROWING AND SCALING YOUR BUSINESS

As your business starts to gain traction and success, the next logical step is to think about growth and scaling. Growing your business can mean increasing your product line, entering new markets, recruiting more staff, and forming strategic partnerships. This chapter will provide

- detailed strategies for business expansion,
- adding new products or services,
- entering new markets,
- recruiting and managing employees, and
- Forming strategic partnerships.

Strategies for Business Expansion

What Are Effective Strategies for Growing a Business?

Growing a business requires careful planning and execution. Effective strategies for business expansion include:

1. **Market Penetration**: Increasing market share within existing markets by promoting current products or services more aggressively.
2. **Market Development**: Entering new markets with current products or services to reach new customers.
3. **Product Development**: Innovating and introducing new products or

services to meet the evolving needs of your market.

4. **Diversification**: Expanding into new markets with new products or services to spread risk and open new revenue streams.

5. **Strategic Partnerships**: Forming alliances with other businesses to leverage their strengths and reach a broader audience.

How To Identify the Right Time to Expand

Identifying the right time to expand is crucial for sustainable growth. Signs that it may be time to expand include:

1. **Consistent Profits**: Your business has been consistently profitable for an extended period.

2. **Market Demand**: There is increasing demand for your products or services.

3. **Operational Efficiency**: Your business operations are efficient, and you can handle additional volume.

4. **Financial Stability**: You have a strong financial foundation and access to capital for expansion.

5. **Clear Opportunities**: You have identified clear opportunities for growth, such as untapped markets or new product lines.

Checklist for Business Expansion

Evaluate Financial Health

- Review financial statements and profitability.
- Ensure access to sufficient capital.

Assess Market Demand

- Conduct market research to evaluate demand.
- Identify trends and customer needs.

Analyze Operational Capacity

- Ensure operational efficiency and capacity.
- Plan for increased production or service delivery.

Identify Growth Opportunities

- Look for untapped markets or customer segments.
- Consider new product or service lines.

Develop a Growth Strategy

- Choose appropriate growth strategies (market penetration, development, product innovation).
- Create a detailed plan and timeline.

Prepare for Challenges

- Identify potential risks and challenges.
- Develop contingency plans.

Adding New Products or Services

How Can Businesses Successfully Introduce New Products or Services?

Introducing new products or services involves thorough research, planning, and execution. Here are the steps to successfully introduce new products or services:

Market Research

- Conduct market research to identify customer needs and preferences.
- Analyze competitors and identify gaps in the market.

Idea Generation

- Brainstorm and generate ideas for new products or services.
- Evaluate ideas based on feasibility, market demand, and alignment with business goals.

Concept Development and Testing

- Develop detailed concepts for the most promising ideas.
- Test concepts with potential customers to gather feedback and refine the product or service.

Business Analysis

- Conduct a business analysis to assess the financial viability of the new product or service.
- Develop a business case and forecast potential revenue and costs.

Product Development

- Create prototypes or samples of the new product.
- Test and refine the product based on feedback.

Market Testing

- Launch the product in a limited market to test its performance.
- Gather feedback and make necessary adjustments.

Commercialization

- Develop a marketing and launch plan.
- Roll out the product or service to the broader market.

What Factors Should Be Considered During This Process?

When introducing new products or services, consider the following factors:

1. **Customer Needs**: Ensure the new product or service meets a genuine need or solves a problem for your customers.
2. **Market Potential**: Evaluate the market potential and demand for the new offering.
3. **Competitor Analysis**: Understand the competitive landscape and identify your unique value proposition.
4. **Cost and Pricing**: Determine the costs involved in development and production and set a competitive price.
5. **Resource Allocation**: Ensure you have the necessary resources (financial, human, and operational) to support the new product or service.
6. **Marketing Strategy**: Develop a comprehensive marketing strategy to promote the new offering and reach your target audience.

Guide for Product and Service Expansion

Conduct Market Research

- Identify customer needs and preferences.
- Analyze competitors and market gaps.

Generate Ideas

- Brainstorm potential products or services.
- Evaluate ideas based on feasibility and demand.

Develop and Test Concepts

- Create detailed product concepts.
- Test with potential customers for feedback.

Analyze Business Viability

- Conduct financial analysis and forecasting.
- Develop a business case.

Develop the Product

- Create prototypes or samples.
- Test and refine the product.

Test the Market

- Launch in a limited market.
- Gather feedback and adjust.

Commercialize the Product

- Develop a marketing and launch plan.
- Roll out to the broader market.

Entering New Markets

What Steps Are Involved in Entering New Markets?

Entering new markets involves strategic planning and thorough research. Here are the steps involved:

Market Research

- Conduct comprehensive market research to understand the target market.
- Analyze market size, growth potential, and customer demographics.

Market Entry Strategy

- Develop a market entry strategy based on your research.
- Consider different entry modes (e.g., direct exporting, partnerships, franchising).

Competitive Analysis

- Analyze the competitive landscape in the new market.
- Identify your unique value proposition and differentiators.

Regulatory Compliance

- Understand and comply with local regulations and requirements.
- Obtain necessary licenses and permits.

Localization

- Adapt your products or services to meet local preferences and cultural nuances.
- Customize marketing materials and messaging for the local market.

Distribution and Logistics

- Establish distribution channels and logistics to ensure product availability.
- Consider partnerships with local distributors or agents.

Marketing and Promotion

- Develop a marketing plan tailored to the new market.
- Use local marketing channels and strategies to reach your audience.

How Can Businesses Assess Market Potential?

Assessing market potential involves evaluating several key factors:

1. **Market Size and Growth**: Analyze the market size and growth rate to determine the potential customer base.
2. **Customer Needs and Preferences**: Understand the needs and preferences of the target market.
3. **Competitive Landscape**: Assess the level of competition and identify your competitive advantages.
4. **Economic and Political Environment**: Evaluate the economic stability and political climate of the target market.
5. **Cultural Differences**: Consider cultural differences and how they may impact your product or service.

Checklist for Market Entry

Conduct Market Research

- Analyze market size, growth, and demographics.
- Identify customer needs and preferences.

Develop a Market Entry Strategy

- Choose an entry mode (direct exporting, partnerships, franchising).
- Create a detailed entry plan.

Analyze Competition

- Study competitors and identify differentiators.
- Develop a unique value proposition.

Ensure Regulatory Compliance

- Understand local regulations and requirements.
- Obtain necessary licenses and permits.

Localize Products and Services

- Adapt products to local preferences.
- Customize marketing materials.

Establish Distribution Channels

- Set up distribution and logistics.
- Partner with local distributors or agents.

Develop Marketing Plan

- Tailor marketing strategies to the local market.
- Use local marketing channels.

Recruiting and Managing Employees

What Are the Best Practices for Hiring New Employees?

Hiring new employees is a critical step in scaling your business. Best practices for hiring include:

Define Job Requirements

- Clearly define the roles and responsibilities of the position.
- Identify the skills and qualifications needed.

Create a Job Description

- Write a detailed job description outlining the role, responsibilities, and qualifications.
- Include information about company culture and benefits.

Source Candidates

- Use multiple channels to source candidates (e.g., job boards, social media, recruitment agencies).
- Consider employee referrals and networking.

Screen Applications

- Review applications and resumes to shortlist candidates.
- Use criteria such as experience, skills, and cultural fit.

Conduct Interviews

- Conduct structured interviews to assess candidates.
- Use a combination of behavioral and technical questions.

Check References

- Verify candidates' backgrounds and references.
- Confirm their previous employment and performance.

Make an Offer

- Extend a job offer to the selected candidate.
- Clearly outline the terms and conditions of employment.

How Can Businesses Effectively Manage and Retain Their Staff?

Effective management and retention of staff involve creating a positive work environment, offering growth opportunities, and recognizing employee contributions. Here are some strategies:

Onboarding and Training

- Provide a comprehensive onboarding program for new employees.
- Offer continuous training and development opportunities.

Performance Management

- Set clear performance goals and expectations.
- Conduct regular performance reviews and provide feedback.

Employee Engagement

- Foster a positive work culture and encourage open communication.
- Recognize and reward employee achievements.

Career Development

- Offer career development and advancement opportunities.
- Support employees' professional growth through training and mentor-ship.

Work-Life Balance

- Promote a healthy work-life balance by offering flexible work arrange-ments.
- Provide benefits that support employees' well-being.

Competitive Compensation

- Offer competitive salaries and benefits to attract and retain talent.
- Regularly review and adjust compensation packages.

Guide for Employee Recruitment and Management

Define Job Requirements

- Identify roles and responsibilities.
- Determine necessary skills and qualifications.

Create Job Description

- Outline role, responsibilities, and qualifications.
- Highlight company culture and benefits.

Source Candidates

- Use job boards, social media, and recruitment agencies.
- Encourage employee referrals.

Screen Applications

- Shortlist candidates based on experience and skills.
- Consider cultural fit.

Conduct Interviews

- Use structured interviews with behavioral and technical questions.
- Assess candidates thoroughly.

Check References

- Verify background and references.
- Confirm previous employment and performance.

Onboarding and Training

- Provide a comprehensive onboarding program.
- Offer continuous training and development.

Performance Management

- Set clear goals and expectations.

- Conduct regular performance reviews.

Employee Engagement

- Foster a positive work culture.
- Recognize and reward achievements.

Career Development

- Offer advancement opportunities.
- Support professional growth.

Work-Life Balance

- Promote flexible work arrangements.
- Provide well-being benefits.

Competitive Compensation

- Offer competitive salaries and benefits.
- Regularly review and adjust compensation.

Forming Strategic Partnerships

Why Are Strategic Partnerships Important?

Strategic partnerships are collaborations between businesses that leverage each other's strengths to achieve mutual benefits. These partnerships can lead to increased market reach, shared resources, and enhanced capabilities. Key benefits of strategic partnerships include:

1. **Access to New Markets**: Partnerships can help you enter new markets and reach new customer segments.
2. **Shared Resources**: Partners can share resources such as technology,

expertise, and distribution networks.

3. **Enhanced Capabilities**: Collaborating with partners can enhance your business's capabilities and competitiveness.

4. **Risk Mitigation**: Sharing risks and costs with partners can reduce the financial burden and exposure.

5. **Innovation**: Partnerships can foster innovation by combining different perspectives and expertise.

How Can Businesses Identify and Form Beneficial Partnerships?

Forming beneficial partnerships involves identifying potential partners, assessing compatibility, and establishing clear terms of collaboration. Here are the steps to form strategic partnerships:

Identify Potential Partners

- Look for businesses with complementary strengths and resources.
- Consider partners with similar values and goals.

Evaluate Compatibility

- Assess the compatibility of potential partners based on culture, vision, and operational style.
- Conduct due diligence to evaluate their financial stability and reputation.

Define Partnership Objectives

- Clearly define the objectives and goals of the partnership.
- Ensure alignment of interests and expectations.

Develop a Partnership Agreement

- Create a detailed partnership agreement outlining roles, responsibilities, and terms.

- Include provisions for governance, decision-making, and conflict resolution.

Establish Communication Channels

- Set up regular communication channels to ensure transparency and collaboration.
- Schedule regular meetings and updates.

Monitor and Evaluate

- Continuously monitor the partnership's progress and performance.
- Evaluate the partnership's impact and make adjustments as needed.

Checklist for Forming Strategic Partnerships

Identify Potential Partners

- Look for complementary strengths and resources.
- Consider similar values and goals.

Evaluate Compatibility

- Assess cultural and operational compatibility.
- Conduct due diligence on financial stability and reputation.

Define Objectives

- Clearly define partnership objectives and goals.
- Ensure alignment of interests.

Develop Agreement

- Create a detailed partnership agreement.
- Include roles, responsibilities, and terms.

Establish Communication

- Set up regular communication channels.
- Schedule regular meetings and updates.

Monitor and Evaluate

- Continuously monitor progress and performance.
- Evaluate impact and make adjustments.

By implementing these strategies for business expansion, adding new products or services, entering new markets, recruiting and managing employees, and forming strategic partnerships, you can effectively grow and scale your business. Use the checklists and guides provided in this chapter to navigate the complexities of business growth and achieve sustainable success.

CHAPTER 12: CONTINUOUS LEARNING AND ADAPTATION

In the dynamic world of business, continuous learning and adaptation are crucial for staying competitive and achieving long-term success. This chapter explores the importance of keeping up with market trends, overcoming common business challenges, the significance of continuous learning, and valuable resources for ongoing education and networking. By embracing these concepts, entrepreneurs can ensure that their businesses remain resilient and innovative.

Keeping Up with Market Trends

Why Is It Important to Stay Updated with Market Trends?

Staying updated with market trends is essential for several reasons:

1. **Informed Decision-Making**: Understanding market trends allows businesses to make informed decisions about product development, marketing strategies, and expansion plans.
2. **Competitive Advantage**: Staying ahead of trends helps businesses anticipate changes and adapt more quickly than competitors.
3. **Customer Insights**: Trends often reflect changing customer preferences and behaviors, enabling businesses to meet their needs better.
4. **Risk Management**: Awareness of market shifts can help businesses identify potential risks and develop strategies to mitigate them.

5. **Innovation**: Keeping up with trends fosters innovation by exposing businesses to new ideas and technologies.

How To Keep Track of Industry Changes

Tracking industry changes involves a proactive approach to gathering and analyzing information. Here are some effective methods:

Industry Publications and Blogs

- Subscribe to industry-specific magazines, journals, and blogs to receive regular updates and expert insights.
- Examples include Harvard Business Review, Forbes, and industry-specific publications.

Market Research Reports

- Purchase or subscribe to market research reports from firms like Gartner, Nielsen, and IBISWorld.
- These reports provide comprehensive data and analysis on industry trends and forecasts.

Social Media and Online Communities

- Follow industry leaders, influencers, and companies on social media platforms like LinkedIn, Twitter, and Facebook.
- Join online communities and forums related to your industry to engage in discussions and stay informed.

Networking and Industry Events

- Attend conferences, trade shows, and networking events to gain insights and connect with industry professionals.
- Participate in webinars and virtual events to stay updated from anywhere.

Google Alerts and RSS Feeds

- Set up Google Alerts for keywords related to your industry to receive notifications about relevant news and updates.
- Use RSS feeds to aggregate content from multiple sources into one place for easy access.

Resources for Staying Informed About Market Trends

Industry Publications

- Harvard Business Review
- Forbes
- Industry-specific magazines and journals

Market Research Firms

- Gartner
- Nielsen
- IBISWorld

Social Media Platforms

- LinkedIn
- Twitter
- Facebook

Online Communities and Forums

- Reddit (industry-specific subreddits)
- Quora
- Specialized forums and groups

Networking and Events

- Conferences and trade shows
- Webinars and virtual events

Google Alerts and RSS Feeds

- Set up Google Alerts for industry keywords
- Use RSS feeds for content aggregation

Overcoming Common Business Challenges

What Are Common Challenges Faced by Businesses?

Businesses of all sizes and stages face a variety of challenges. Some common challenges include:

Financial Management

- Managing cash flow, budgeting, and securing funding.
- Addressing unexpected expenses and financial setbacks.

Market Competition

- Competing with established players and new entrants.
- Differentiating your products or services in a crowded market.

Customer Acquisition and Retention

- Attracting new customers and retaining existing ones.
- Managing customer expectations and delivering consistent value.

Regulatory Compliance

- Navigating complex regulations and legal requirements.
- Ensuring compliance with industry standards and laws.

Technology Adoption

- Keeping up with technological advancements and integrating new tools.
- Managing cybersecurity risks and data privacy concerns.

Scaling Operations

- Managing growth and scaling business operations effectively.
- Maintaining quality and efficiency during expansion.

How Can These Challenges Be Effectively Addressed?

Addressing business challenges requires strategic planning, adaptability, and a proactive approach. Here are strategies to tackle common challenges:

Financial Management

- Implement robust financial planning and budgeting processes.
- Use accounting software to track income and expenses.
- Explore diverse funding sources, such as loans, grants, and investors.

Market Competition

- Conduct thorough market research to understand competitors and customer needs.
- Focus on innovation and continuous improvement of products or services.
- Develop a strong brand identity and unique value proposition.

Customer Acquisition and Retention

- Invest in marketing and sales strategies to attract new customers.

- Provide exceptional customer service to build loyalty and retention.
- Use customer feedback to improve products and services continuously.

Regulatory Compliance

- Stay informed about relevant regulations and industry standards.
- Consult with legal and compliance experts to ensure adherence.
- Implement compliance management systems and regular audits.

Technology Adoption

- Keep abreast of technological trends and advancements.
- Invest in training and development to build tech-savvy teams.
- Implement cybersecurity measures and data protection protocols.

Scaling Operations

- Develop scalable business processes and systems.
- Focus on efficient resource allocation and management.
- Monitor key performance indicators (KPIs) to ensure growth aligns with goals.

Checklist for Problem-Solving in Business

Identify the Problem

- Clearly define the problem and its impact on the business.
- Gather relevant data and insights.

Analyze the Problem

- Conduct a root cause analysis to understand underlying issues.
- Use tools like SWOT analysis and Pareto analysis.

Develop Solutions

- Brainstorm potential solutions and evaluate their feasibility.
- Consider short-term and long-term solutions.

Implement the Solution

- Develop an action plan with clear steps and responsibilities.
- Communicate the plan to relevant stakeholders.

Monitor and Evaluate

- Track the implementation process and measure results.
- Make adjustments as needed based on feedback and performance.

Document and Learn

- Document the problem-solving process and outcomes.
- Share lessons learned with the team to prevent future issues.

Importance of Continuous Learning

Why Is Continuous Learning Vital for Business Success?

Continuous learning is essential for business success for several reasons:

1. **Adaptability**: The business landscape is constantly evolving, and continuous learning helps businesses stay adaptable and responsive to changes.
2. **Innovation**: Learning new skills and knowledge fosters innovation and keeps businesses competitive.
3. **Skill Development**: Continuous learning helps employees and leaders develop new skills and improve existing ones, enhancing overall performance.

4. **Problem-Solving**: Learning from experiences and challenges equips businesses with better problem-solving capabilities.
5. **Employee Engagement**: Providing learning opportunities boosts employee morale, engagement, and retention.

What Resources Are Available for Ongoing Education?

Numerous resources are available for ongoing education, including:

Online Courses and Webinars

- Platforms like Coursera, Udemy, and LinkedIn Learning offer a wide range of courses on business, technology, and soft skills.
- Participate in webinars hosted by industry experts and organizations.

Books and E-books

- Read books by industry leaders, business experts, and thought leaders.
- Access e-books and audiobooks for convenient learning.

Professional Associations

- Join professional associations and organizations related to your industry.
- Attend conferences, workshops, and networking events.

Mentorship and Coaching

- Seek mentorship from experienced professionals in your field.
- Consider hiring business coaches for personalized guidance.

Podcasts and Videos

- Listen to podcasts and watch videos on topics relevant to your business.
- Subscribe to industry experts' channels and podcasts.

Academic Institutions

- Enroll in courses and programs offered by universities and colleges.
- Consider pursuing certifications and advanced degrees.

How Can Networking Benefit Business Growth?

Networking offers numerous benefits for business growth:

1. **Knowledge Sharing**: Networking allows you to exchange knowledge, ideas, and best practices with other professionals.
2. **Opportunities**: Networking can lead to new business opportunities, partnerships, and collaborations.
3. **Support and Advice**: Building a network of trusted contacts provides access to support, advice, and mentorship.
4. **Visibility**: Networking increases your visibility and reputation within your industry.
5. **Market Insights**: Engaging with peers and industry leaders helps you stay informed about market trends and developments.

Tips for Effective Networking and Professional Development

Attend Events Regularly

- Participate in industry conferences, trade shows, and networking events.
- Engage in webinars and virtual events for remote networking.

Be Genuine and Approachable

- Approach networking with a genuine interest in building relationships.
- Be approachable, friendly, and open to conversations.

Listen Actively

- Listen to others and show interest in their experiences and insights.
- Ask questions and engage in meaningful conversations.

Follow Up

- Follow up with new contacts after networking events.
- Send personalized messages or emails to continue the conversation.

Offer Value

- Offer your knowledge, skills, and resources to help others.
- Build a reputation as someone who adds value to their network.

Leverage Social Media

- Use LinkedIn and other professional networks to connect with industry peers.
- Share valuable content and engage with your network online.

Join Professional Associations

- Become a member of professional associations related to your industry.
- Participate in association events and activities.

Seek Mentorship

- Find mentors who can provide guidance and support.
- Be open to mentoring others and sharing your knowledge.

By staying updated with market trends, overcoming common business challenges, embracing continuous learning, and leveraging valuable resources for education and networking, you can ensure your business remains competitive and adaptable. Use the tips and checklists provided in this chapter to enhance your knowledge, build strong networks, and drive your business toward sustained success.

CHAPTER 13: REAL-WORLD SUCCESS STORIES AND FINAL THOUGHTS

Inspirational Entrepreneurial Journeys

1. Sara Blakely – Spanx

Sara Blakely, the founder of Spanx, started her journey with a simple idea: creating footless pantyhose. She faced numerous rejections from manufacturers and investors, but her persistence paid off when she convinced a manufacturer to produce her product. Spanx became a multimillion-dollar company, and Blakely was named the world's youngest self-made female billionaire by Forbes in 2012.

2. Elon Musk – Tesla and SpaceX

Elon Musk's journey is a testament to the power of vision and resilience. Despite facing significant challenges and near-bankruptcy, Musk persisted with his vision for electric vehicles and space exploration. Today, Tesla and SpaceX are industry leaders, revolutionizing their respective fields.

3. Oprah Winfrey – OWN Network

Oprah Winfrey's story is about overcoming adversity. Rising from poverty and a troubled childhood, she became a global media mogul. Her determination and focus on authenticity and connection with her audience have made her a household name and a powerful businesswoman.

What Lessons Can Be Learned from Their Experiences?

1. **Persistence Pays Off**: Entrepreneurs like Sara Blakely and Elon Musk faced numerous setbacks but did not give up. Persistence and resilience are crucial traits for any successful entrepreneur.
2. **Innovation and Vision**: Having a clear vision and the willingness to innovate can set entrepreneurs apart. Musk's vision for sustainable energy and space exploration has driven his success.
3. **Authenticity**: Oprah Winfrey's authentic connection with her audience has been a significant factor in her success. Building trust and being genuine can create a loyal customer base.

Actionable Insights from Their Journeys

1. **Believe in Your Idea**: Trust your instincts and be prepared to defend your idea even when faced with scepticism.
2. **Be Prepared for Rejections**: Understand that rejection is part of the journey. Use it as a learning experience and motivation to improve.
3. **Stay Focused on Your Vision**: Keep your long-term vision in mind and make decisions that align with your ultimate goals.

Lessons from Failures and Triumphs

Highlight Key Lessons from Both Failures and Successes

1. The Failure of Kodak

Kodak, once a giant in the photography industry, failed to adapt to the digital revolution. Despite inventing the first digital camera, the company did not capitalize on it, leading to its bankruptcy in 2012. The lesson here is the importance of innovation and adapting to market changes.

2. The Success of Airbnb

Airbnb started as a simple idea to rent out air mattresses in a living room.

Today, it's a global platform disrupting the hospitality industry. The key to their success was identifying a market gap and leveraging technology to scale their operations.

How Can These Lessons Be Applied to New Businesses?

1. **Adaptability**: Be willing to pivot and adapt to market changes. Staying rigid can lead to missed opportunities.
2. **Identify Market Gaps**: Look for unmet needs in the market and create solutions that address those gaps.
3. **Leverage Technology**: Use technology to streamline operations and reach a broader audience.

Case Studies of Both Failures and Successes

Case Study: Blockbuster vs. Netflix

Blockbuster failed to adapt to the rise of digital streaming, while Netflix embraced the change. Today, Netflix is a global leader in entertainment, while Blockbuster is a cautionary tale of the dangers of complacency.

Insights from Experienced Business Owners

Richard Branson – Virgin Group

- **Advice**: "Business opportunities are like buses; there's always another one coming." This highlights the importance of staying alert and ready to seize new opportunities.

Sheryl Sandberg – Facebook

- **Advice**: "Done is better than perfect." This emphasizes the value of taking action and iterating rather than waiting for perfection.

Mark Cuban – Entrepreneur and Investor

- **Advice**: "Sales cure all." Focusing on generating revenue and building a strong sales strategy is crucial for business survival and growth.

What Common Themes Emerge from Their Experiences?

1. **Action-Oriented**: Successful entrepreneurs prioritize taking action over endless planning.
2. **Customer Focus**: A deep understanding of customer needs and a commitment to customer satisfaction are common themes.
3. **Adaptability and Resilience**: The ability to adapt to changes and bounce back from setbacks is essential.

Practical Tips from Experienced Business Owners

1. **Focus on Sales**: Ensure your business model has a strong sales strategy.
2. **Customer Feedback**: Regularly seek and act on customer feedback to improve your offerings.
3. **Stay Flexible**: Be open to change and ready to pivot your business model as needed.

Recap of Key Takeaways

The Most Important Points Covered in this Book

1. **Mindset Matters**: Building a success-oriented mindset is fundamental for entrepreneurial success.
2. **Planning is Crucial**: A well-crafted business plan is a roadmap to success.
3. **Financial Management**: Effective financial management and budgeting are essential for sustainability.
4. **Marketing and Branding**: Strong branding and effective marketing

strategies drive customer acquisition and retention.

5. **Continuous Learning**: Staying informed and continuously learning keeps your business competitive.

How To Apply These Takeaways to Your Businesses

1. **Develop a Strong Vision**: Define your business vision and align your strategies with it.
2. **Create a Detailed Business Plan**: Use the templates and checklists provided to develop a comprehensive business plan.
3. **Focus on Financial Health**: Implement effective financial management practices and regularly review your financial performance.
4. **Invest in Marketing**: Develop a robust marketing strategy to reach and engage your target audience.
5. **Embrace Continuous Learning**: Use the recommended resources to stay updated and improve your skills.

Checklist of Key Takeaways

Mindset Development

- Cultivate resilience and a positive mindset.
- Set clear goals and stay focused.

Business Planning

- Develop a comprehensive business plan.
- Regularly review and update your plan.

Financial Management

- Monitor cash flow and manage expenses.
- Use financial tools to track performance.

Marketing and Branding

- Create a strong brand identity.
- Implement effective marketing strategies.

Continuous Learning

- Stay updated with industry trends.
- Invest in ongoing education and professional development.

Encouragement for Aspiring Entrepreneurs

Offer Motivational Messages to Inspire Readers

1. **Believe in Yourself**: Confidence is key. Trust in your abilities and vision.
2. **Embrace Failure**: Every setback is an opportunity to learn and grow.
3. **Stay Persistent**: Success often comes after many attempts. Keep pushing forward.

Steps Take to Start Your Entrepreneurial Journey

1. **Identify Your Passion**: Choose a business idea that aligns with your interests and strengths.
2. **Conduct Market Research**: Understand your market and identify opportunities.
3. **Develop a Business Plan**: Create a detailed plan to guide your business journey.
4. **Secure Funding**: Explore funding options and secure the necessary capital.
5. **Launch and Iterate**: Start your business, gather feedback, and continuously improve.

APPENDICES

The appendices section is designed to provide you with essential tools and resources that will support you on your entrepreneurial journey. From checklists and templates to a glossary of business terms, recommended reading, and online tools, this section will serve as a comprehensive reference guide to help you navigate the complexities of starting and running a business.

Essential Checklists and Templates

Business Startup Checklist
Idea Validation

- Conduct market research
- Identify target audience
- Validate the demand for your product/service

Business Planning

- Write a business plan
- Define your business model
- Create financial projections

Legal Setup

- Choose a business structure (LLC, Corporation, etc.)
- Register your business name
- Obtain necessary licenses and permits

- Apply for an Employer Identification Number (EIN)

Funding and Finances

- Determine startup costs
- Explore funding options (loans, investors, grants)
- Set up a business bank account
- Implement accounting and bookkeeping systems

Branding and Marketing

- Develop a brand identity (logo, colors, fonts)
- Create a marketing plan
- Build a website and social media presence
- Plan your initial marketing campaigns

Operations

- Set up your office or workspace
- Source suppliers and vendors
- Establish business processes and workflows

Launch Preparation

- Test your product/service
- Plan your launch event or campaign
- Gather customer feedback and make improvements

Financial Projection Template
Financial ProjectionYear 1Year 2Year 3
Revenue

Cost of Goods Sold

Gross Profit

Operating Expenses

Net Profit

Cash Flow

Marketing Plan Template

Executive Summary

- Overview of your marketing objectives and strategies

Market Research

- Analysis of industry, market, and competitors
- Identification of target audience

Marketing Goals

- Define specific, measurable, achievable, relevant, and time-bound (SMART) goals

Marketing Strategies

- Product strategy
- Pricing strategy
- Promotion strategy
- Place (distribution) strategy

Marketing Tactics

- Social media campaigns
- Content marketing
- Email marketing
- Paid advertising (Google Ads, Facebook Ads)

Budget and Resources

- Allocation of marketing budget
- Required resources (tools, personnel)

Evaluation and Metrics

- Key performance indicators (KPIs)
- Methods for measuring and analyzing results

Glossary of Business Terms

1. **Asset**: Any resource owned by a business that has economic value.
2. **Balance Sheet**: A financial statement that summarizes a company's assets, liabilities, and shareholders' equity at a specific point in time.
3. **Brand Identity**: The visible elements of a brand, such as color, design, and logo, that distinguish it from competitors.
4. **Cash Flow**: The net amount of cash being transferred into and out of a business.
5. **Customer Segmentation**: The process of dividing a customer base into distinct groups based on specific criteria.
6. **Digital Marketing**: The use of digital channels, such as social media, email, and websites, to promote a product or service.
7. **EIN (Employer Identification Number)**: A unique identifier assigned to a business by the IRS for tax purposes.
8. **Market Research**: The process of gathering, analyzing, and interpreting information about a market, including information about the target audience and competitors.
9. **MVP (Minimum Viable Product)**: A product with the minimum features necessary to validate a business idea and gather customer feedback.
10. **SWOT Analysis**: A strategic planning tool that evaluates a business's strengths, weaknesses, opportunities, and threats.

Online Tools and Additional Materials

Financial Management

1. **QuickBooks**: An accounting software package developed and marketed by Intuit, suitable for small and medium-sized businesses.
2. **Xero**: An easy-to-use online accounting software for small businesses.
3. **Wave Accounting**: A free accounting software that includes invoicing and receipt scanning.

Project Management

1. **Trello**: A project management tool that uses boards, lists, and cards to organize tasks.
2. **Asana**: A web and mobile application designed to help teams organize, track, and manage their work.
3. **Monday.com**: A project management tool that helps teams plan, organize, and track work in one visual, collaborative space.

Marketing

1. **Google Analytics**: Google offers a web analytics service that tracks and reports website traffic.
2. **Hootsuite**: A social media management platform that allows users to schedule and manage social media posts.
3. **Mailchimp**: An email marketing service that enables users to create, send, and analyze email campaigns.

BONUS

Discover the Secrets to Entrepreneurial Success!

Are you ready to transform your dreams into reality and become a successful entrepreneur? This book is a bonus to you for purchasing this one!

Each day brings new opportunities and challenges, and you have the tools and mindset to seize them and thrive.

But do you ever wonder:

- How can I build the right mindset for success?
- How do I strategically plan for my business's future?

This book is your key to unlocking these answers and more.
What You'll Learn:

Cultivating a Success-Oriented Mindset:

- Understand the essence of an entrepreneurial mindset.
- Overcome limiting beliefs and fears with practical strategies.
- Build resilience and adaptability for long-term success.

Setting Clear and Achievable Goals:

- Discover the power of effective goal setting.
- Learn how to set SMART goals that align with your vision.
- Utilize techniques to set and achieve effective goals.

Strategic Planning Fundamentals:

- Grasp the basics of strategic planning.
- Develop a compelling vision and mission statement.
- Craft a comprehensive strategic plan with actionable steps.

Building and Testing Your Minimum Viable Product (MVP):

- Understand the MVP concept and its significance.
- Follow the steps to develop and launch your MVP.
- Iterate and improve your product based on feedback.

Effective Time and Financial Management:

- Master time management techniques to boost productivity.
- Set up an efficient accounting system for your business.
- Manage cash flow and business expenses effectively.

Continuous Learning and Strong Customer Relationships:

- Embrace continuous learning for business success.
- Stay updated with market trends and industry changes.
- Develop strong customer relationships and create loyal advocates.

Practical Tools and Resources:

- Worksheets and templates to help you apply the concepts learned.
- Quizzes to assess your understanding and readiness for entrepreneurial success.

Why This Book Stands Out:

- Practical Steps and Checklists: Clear, actionable steps and checklists guide you through every stage.

- Simple Language: Easy-to-understand content, free from complex jargon.
- Real-Life Examples: Insights from the experiences of successful entrepreneurs.
- Tools and Resources: Worksheets, templates, and other resources to help you implement what you learn.

Download your FREE bonus here:

Or Scan the code below to access your bonus. Happy reading.

I will also appreciate your Honest Reviews.

Before you go, I have one quick request.

    If this book helped you—even in a small way—could you take 60 seconds to leave a review?

It helps more people like you find this and actually take action instead of staying stuck.

    You don't need to write anything long. Just share:

- **What you found helpful**
- **What stood out**
- **Or what you're planning to do next**

Leave your review here

Or Scan the QR Code

- Open Your Camera app
- Point Your Mobile device at the QR Code below
- The Review Page appear in your web browser.

I read every single review, and I truly appreciate yours.

Thank you for being part of this journey—and for helping others discover what you just learned.

References

https://www.forbes.com/global/2012/0326/billionaires-12-feature-united-states-spanx-sara-blakely-american-booty.html

https://medium.com/@baranserhatozer/drew-houston-the-mastermind-behind-dropbox-lessons-from-his-epic-journey-2d10c4902a58

https://www.founderstoday.news/success-story-of-craigslist/

https://medium.com/@tanyaagarwal9812/the-pioneering-journey-of-airbnb-founders-brian-chesky-nathan-blecharczyk-and-joe-gebbia-7306ab186f2b

https://www.elephantlearning.com/post/colonel-sanders-rejected-over-one-thousand-times-before-starting-kfc

https://fs.blog/carol-dweck-mindset/

https://stories.starbucks.com/leadership/howard-schultz/

https://www.britannica.com/money/Howard-Schultz

https://mailchimp.com/about/founders/

https://www.cnbc.com/2017/01/09/ceo-of-billion-dollar-company-gopro-shares-his-secret-to-success.html

https://www.timefordesigns.com/blog/2023/10/05/the-rise-and-fall-of-bl
ockbuster-a-cautionary-tale-in-digital-transformation/

https://www.linkedin.com/pulse/from-setbacks-success-inspiring-journey
-elon-musk-siva-ganapathi

https://www.linkedin.com/pulse/from-adversity-triumph-inspiring-journ
ey-oprah-winfrey-mano-ranjith-b6evc

https://www.linkedin.com/pulse/how-photo-giant-failed-see-digital-pict
ure-kodak-michael-effanga

https://www.linkedin.com/pulse/from-air-mattresses-global-phenomeno
n-airbnb-case-study-farabi

www.ingramcontent.com/pod-product-compliance
Lightning Source LLC
Chambersburg PA
CBHW020435240526
45479CB00017B/1319